Strength & Beauty
the Book of Ruth

Garry Glaub

Copyright © 2014 by Garry Glaub

Strength & Beauty: the Book of Ruth
by Garry Glaub

Printed in the United States of America

ISBN #: 978-0-9847533-2-1

All rights reserved solely by the publisher. The author guarantees all contents are original and do not infringe upon the legal rights of any other person or work. No part of this work may be reproduced in any form without the permission of the author. The views expressed in this book are not necessarily those of the publisher.

Unless otherwise indicated, and in Chapters 1-5, "Scripture quotations taken from the New American Standard Bible®, Copyright © 1960, 1962, 1963, 1968, 1971, 1972, 1973, 1975, 1977, 1995 by The Lockman Foundation Used by permission." (www.Lockman.org)

Chapter 6-7: "Scripture taken from the New King James Version®. Copyright © 1982 by Thomas Nelson, Inc. Used by permission. All rights reserved."

Cover Photo taken by Garry Glaub in Petra, Jordan, March 28, 2006.

Table of Contents:

Preface:	Page 11
Chapter 1: There's a Lot Going on in Moab	Page 15
Chapter 2: From Pleasure to Bitterness	Page 25
Chapter 3: Barley, Wheat and Grapes	Page 39
Chapter 4: Strangers in a Strange Land	Page 59
Chapter 5: There is a Redeemer	Page 65
Chapter 6: I've Been Redeemed	Page 79
Chapter 7: By the Blood of the Lamb	Page 91
Acknowledgements:	Page 109

Dedication:

[13] For He rescued us from the domain of darkness, and transferred us to the kingdom of His beloved Son [14] in whom we have redemption, the forgiveness of sins.
Colossians 1:13-14 (NASB)

To the One who set the captives free, and who redeemed me! The Bible reminds us how we can demonstrate our love for Him, by keeping His commandments. Jesus summed up those commandments by telling us to love Him with all of our heart, soul, mind and strength, and to love our neighbor as ourselves. It sounds like we are to be completely sold out for Him. LORD, help me to love You the way You deserve to be loved!

Preface:

In the Bible, there is not a subject more important or pervasive than redemption. Simply speaking, redemption is the act of purchasing back an item that has been sold. A price must be paid to return that item to the original possessor. Without God, the Bible tells us that we are slaves to sin. Picture the slave market of the pre-Civil War era in Charleston, South Carolina, and while you're at it, picture yourself on display for all to purchase. We could be purchased by the cruelest slave owner, who will work us to the bone, whip us when we trip and will be responsible for our lives and certainly, our deaths. But then a buyer comes in and outbids the rest. Instead of harming us, he sets us free. Though we are free, we are so astounded by his amazing act of love that we choose to serve him, for the rest of our lives. Because he loved us first, we now love him, and his love was more than just a word. It came with the greatest action.

That is what God did for each of us. To cut the bonds of slavery, Jesus came and set the captives free. Because God tells us that there can be no forgiveness of sin without the spilling of innocent blood, Jesus became our Passover Lamb. He died for our sins, and if we repent of our sins and believe on Him as our Messiah, we receive the reward for His perfect life, just as He received the death for our imperfect lives! What a great trade for us, but what an awesome cost for Him! We know how the Father looked upon this sacrifice:

Yet it pleased the LORD to bruise Him.
Isaiah 53:10

It pleased the Father, because through that event, all of us had a chance of a relationship with Him. There was no other way. Jesus prayed three times in the Garden of Gethsemane that if there was any other way, for the Father to allow this cup to pass from Him. Redemption cost Jesus His life, and at the same time, cost the Father and the Son the relationship they had treasured for eternity. When our sins were placed upon the shoulders of Jesus, the Father turned away, as He could not look upon sin. How did Jesus respond? "My God, My God, why have You forsaken Me?" Notice the loss of relationship even in the terminology Jesus used. "MY GOD" still reveals love and knowledge, but the relationship of "MY FATHER" is noticeably absent. Though salvation is free, we never should lose sight of the cost of our redemption.

Paul says,

[7] In Him we have redemption through His blood, the forgiveness of our trespasses, according to the riches of His grace [8] which He lavished on us.
Ephesians 1:7-8 (NASB)

The blood of Jesus is the currency for our redemption. Another aspect of redemption that we should not forget is that everyone is redeemable! When God called Jonah to go to Nineveh, Jonah ran in the opposite direction. He got on a boat headed to Tarshish, and when his shipmates began to see the storm ravaging the boat as a direct result of Jonah's fight with the LORD, they threw him overboard. Swallowed by a large fish, Jonah spent three days in that darkness. Eventually, he found his way to Nineveh, shared the gospel, and amazingly all of the Ninevites began to follow the LORD! This did not please Jonah, sadly, as he wanted God to punish his enemies, not forgive them. Each of us tends to have a Nineveh in our lives, as well, but we need to remember, each of us were likely that "Nineveh" in someone else's life before God redeemed us.

Each person who we see stumbling in sin should not receive our judgment, but our love, for their lives mirror ours. Before God saved us, we were shackled by a ball and chain to that life of sin. The name Jesus means, "God is salvation," and without that salvation, we are all lost. In fact, we all deserve to be lost, but by His grace, we have been redeemed!

This beautiful romance at the beginning of the history books of the Old Testament tells a tale of Ruth, from Moab. Through this book, we can glean more than the fields of Boaz; we can glean about our own redemption! With discussion questions at the end of each chapter, this book is a wonderful, 7-week small group study, yet it also can recharge your personal walk with the One who did so much for all of us.

Feel free to contact me with any questions or concerns: gg4jesus@gmail.com and check out my website at www.garryglaub.com.

Chapter 1, There's a Lot Going on in Moab!

This book is one of the gems of the Old Testament. In this sweet tale of life, death, loss, gain and romance, there is a subtle foreshadowing of the life each believer has in Jesus Christ! The first leg of the journey is from Bethlehem to the land of Moab.

[1] **Now it came about in the days when the judges governed, that there was a famine in the land. And a certain man of Bethlehem in Judah went to sojourn in the land of Moab with his wife and his two sons.** [2] **The name of the man was Elimelech, and the name of his wife, Naomi; and the names of his two sons were Mahlon and Chilion, Ephrathites of Bethlehem in Judah. Now they entered the land of Moab and remained there.** [3] **Then Elimelech, Naomi's husband, died; and she was left with her two sons.** [4] **They took for themselves Moabite women as wives; the name of the one was Orpah and the name of the other Ruth. And they lived**

there about ten years.

⁵ Then both Mahlon and Chilion also died, and the woman was bereft of her two children and her husband. ⁶ Then she arose with her daughters-in-law that she might return from the land of Moab, for she had heard in the land of Moab that the Lord had visited His people in giving them food.
⁷ So she departed from the place where she was, and her two daughters-in-law with her; and they went on the way to return to the land of Judah. ⁸ And Naomi said to her two daughters-in-law, "Go, return each of you to her mother's house. May the Lord deal kindly with you as you have dealt with the dead and with me.
⁹ "May the Lord grant that you may find rest, each in the house of her husband." Then she kissed them, and they lifted up their voices and wept. ¹⁰ And they said to her, "No, but we will surely return with you to your people."
¹¹ But Naomi said, "Return, my daughters. Why should you go with me? Have I yet sons in my womb, that they may be your husbands? ¹² "Return, my daughters! Go, for I am too old to have a husband. If I said I have hope, if I should even have a husband tonight and also bear sons,¹³ would you therefore wait until they were grown? Would you therefore refrain from marrying? No, my daughters; for it is harder for me than for you, for the hand of the Lord has gone forth against me."
¹⁴ And they lifted up their voices and wept again; and Orpah kissed her mother-in-law, but Ruth clung to her.¹⁵ Then she said, "Behold, your sister-in-law has gone back to her people and her gods; return after your sister-in-law." ¹⁶ But Ruth said, "Do not urge me to leave you or turn back from following you; for where you go, I will go, and where you lodge, I will lodge. Your people shall be my people, and your God, my God.¹⁷ "Where you die, I will die, and there I will be buried. Thus may the Lord do to me, and worse, if

anything but death parts you and me." ¹⁸ When she saw that she was determined to go with her, she said no more to her. ¹⁹ So they both went until they came to Bethlehem. And when they had come to Bethlehem, all the city was stirred because of them, and the women said, "Is this Naomi?" ²⁰ She said to them, "Do not call me Naomi; call me Mara, for the Almighty has dealt very bitterly with me. ²¹ "I went out full, but the Lord has brought me back empty. Why do you call me Naomi, since the Lord has witnessed against me and the Almighty has afflicted me?" ²² So Naomi returned, and with her Ruth the Moabitess, her daughter-in-law, who returned from the land of Moab. And they came to Bethlehem at the beginning of barley harvest.
Ruth 1:1-22 (NASB)

Though this tale begins in Bethlehem, a town we all should be familiar with as it saw the birth of Jesus, a famine takes the man Elimelech, wife Naomi, and sons Mahlon and Chilion to the land of Moab. Moab would occupy the mountainous region of Jordan today, just east of the Dead Sea. Let's begin with some insight into the foundation of the nation of Moab:

³⁰ Lot went up from Zoar, and stayed in the mountains, and his two daughters with him; for he was afraid to stay in Zoar; and he stayed in a cave, he and his two daughters. ³¹ Then the firstborn said to the younger, "Our father is old, and there is not a man on earth to come in to us after the manner of the earth. ³² "Come, let us make our father drink wine, and let us lie with him that we may preserve our family through our father." ³³ So they made their father drink wine that night, and the firstborn went in and lay with her father; and he did not know when she lay down or when she arose.

³⁴ On the following day, the firstborn said to the younger, "Behold, I lay last night with my father; let us make him drink wine tonight also; then you go in and lie with him, that we may preserve our family through our father."
³⁵ So they made their father drink wine that night also, and the younger arose and lay with him; and he did not know when she lay down or when she arose.
³⁶ Thus both the daughters of Lot were with child by their father. ³⁷ The firstborn bore a son, and called his name Moab; he is the father of the Moabites to this day.
³⁸ As for the younger, she also bore a son, and called his name Ben-ammi; he is the father of the sons of Ammon to this day.
Genesis 19:30-38 (NASB)

The Ammonites and Moabites began with an incestuous relationship between Lot and his daughters. Remember, Lot's wife was no longer with him, having been a-SALTED in a retreat from the Lord's judgment on Sodom and Gomorrah. The unnamed wife had been instructed not to look back at the Lord's wrath, and when she disobediently stole a glance, turned into a pillar of salt. Worried that there were no men to marry, to carry on the family name, Lot's daughters got him drunk and slept with him on consecutive nights. Maybe this was the way they got back at their father for offering his daughter to the sexual deviants outside his door in Sodom, in Lot's attempt to get the Sodomites away from the angel of the Lord! The sons born to Lot's daughters began two nations that continued as the enemies of Israel. Look at this interesting verse written in post-exilic Israel, when the times of the kings had ended, and the southern tribes had returned from 70 years of captivity in Babylon:

¹ On that day they read aloud from the book of Moses in the

hearing of the people; and there was found written in it that no Ammonite or Moabite should ever enter the assembly of God, ² because they did not meet the sons of Israel with bread and water, but hired Balaam against them to curse them. However, our God turned the curse into a blessing. ³ So when they heard the law, they excluded all foreigners from Israel.
Nehemiah 13:1-3 (NASB)

In the verse above, we see the specific reason Ammonites and Moabites were disallowed from entering the assembly of God, and it recounted a tale further explained in Numbers 22. Balaam was a prophet hired by the enemies of Israel. Though he refused to speak words that did not come from God, he encouraged the Ammonites and Moabites to trick the children of Israel, tempting them with their women. In so doing, the children of Israel married foreign wives and fell away from the LORD.

Remember, these nations resulted from this sordid relationship between Lot and his daughters. While it would be simple to blame the daughters, we know the adage concerning leading a horse to water. While the verse says their plan was to "make" their father drink wine, there certainly was no gun put to his head. Lot was certainly stunned after the Lord's complete removal of Sodom and Gomorrah, and as he chose to live in that city while Abraham opted for a more rural setting, Lot may have been in a state of self-doubt and self-blame. But we know that regardless of Lot's mistakes, God views him as "righteous!"

⁴ For if God did not spare angels when they sinned, but cast them into hell and committed them to pits of darkness, reserved for judgment; ⁵ and did not spare the ancient

world, but preserved Noah, a preacher of righteousness, with seven others, when He brought a flood upon the world of the ungodly; [6] and if He condemned the cities of Sodom and Gomorrah to destruction by reducing them to ashes, having made them an example to those who would live ungodly lives thereafter; [7] and if He rescued righteous Lot, oppressed by the sensual conduct of unprincipled men [8] (for by what he saw and heard that righteous man, while living among them, felt his righteous soul tormented day after day by their lawless deeds), [9] then the Lord knows how to rescue the godly from temptation, and to keep the unrighteous under punishment for the day of judgment, [10] and especially those who indulge the flesh in its corrupt desires and despise authority. Daring, self-willed, they do not tremble when they revile angelic majesties, [11] whereas angels who are greater in might and power do not bring a reviling judgment against them before the Lord.
2 Peter 2:4-11 (NASB)

So as our quaint story continues, the setting changes from the famine-ravaged nation of Israel in the time of the judges to the nation of Moab. In Hebrew, Moab means "of the father," and when we complete this story, it will be easy to see the Father's hand!

The family went from bad to worse. Having departed the famine in Bethlehem, Elimelech died In Moab. The sons both married, but before 10 years had elapsed, both of the sons were deceased, as well. That left Naomi with the recent additions to her family, Orpah and Ruth. We all know who has the starring role of those daughters-in-law, as this is not called the Book of Orpah! After seeing two changes in settings already, it is now time for another.

**⁷ So she departed from the place where she was, and her two daughters-in-law with her; and they went on the way to return to the land of Judah.
⁸ And Naomi said to her two daughters-in-law, "Go, return each of you to her mother's house. May the Lord deal kindly with you as you have dealt with the dead and with me. ⁹ "May the Lord grant that you may find rest, each in the house of her husband." Then she kissed them, and they lifted up their voices and wept.
Ruth 1:7-9 (NASB)**

In the simple statement above, we see the godly attributes of Naomi, who even in her loss and mourning was concerned for the lives of the young women, who also were in mourning. By the Law, it was perfectly valid for Naomi to marry again, but having lost her husband and children, she certainly did not see her new life as freedom. In fact, she was feeling abandoned by the Lord, as all the potential breadwinners of the family appeared to be gone. At the same time, she had heard that the famine in Israel had ended, so her return to Israel surely carried the hope of a relative's assistance. At the same time, Naomi urged her daughters-in-law to do the same, and also gave both girls a blessing from the Lord, along with a hope that they both remarry. That spiritual blessing was one of the main differences between Moab and Israel, and Judah specifically. Moab was a nation of idol worship, and though idol worship also occurred in Israel, the Jewish land remained the only nation of God! Both young ladies insisted on going with Naomi and Naomi's response tells us much about this story:

**But Naomi said, "Return, my daughters. Why should you go with me? Have I yet sons in my womb, that they may be your husbands?
Ruth 1:11 (NASB)**

What was Naomi talking about? What would it matter if she was carrying twin sons even then? In the next chapter, we will learn more about the Old Testament laws of redemption, which will help us more fully understand this comment by Ruth.

DISCUSSION QUESTIONS:

1. We read in Nehemiah that there are to be no Moabites or Ammonites in the assembly of the LORD. Is this still in effect today? Are there other groups or nationalities who the LORD excludes from finding Him?
2. Does God view you as righteous? If we are sinners, how can any of us be viewed as righteous?
3. Is Naomi a weak woman or a strong woman? What kind of strength does it take for someone who is otherwise alone to encourage people to depart?
4. Did Naomi love her daughters-in-law? Did they love her?
5. Name some of the ways that Moab and Israel were different.

Notes:

Notes:

Chapter 2,
From Pleasure to Bitterness!

In the previous chapter, Naomi made a comment to her daughters-in-law mentioning the fact that she was not pregnant:

But Naomi said, "Return, my daughters. Why should you go with me? Have I yet sons in my womb, that they may be your husbands?
Ruth 1:11 (NASB)

What was Naomi talking about? What would it matter if she was carrying twin sons even then? This comment points to Levirate marriage and the Old Testament laws of redemption, To better understand this, let's look closer into the life of Judah, one of the 12 sons of Jacob (Israel):

[1] **And it came about at that time, that Judah departed from his brothers and visited a certain Adullamite, whose name was Hirah.** [2] **Judah saw there a daughter of a certain**

Canaanite whose name was Shua; and he took her and went in to her. ³ So she conceived and bore a son and he named him Er. ⁴ Then she conceived again and bore a son and named him Onan. ⁵ She bore still another son and named him Shelah; and it was at Chezib that she bore him. ⁶ Now Judah took a wife for Er his firstborn, and her name was Tamar. ⁷ But Er, Judah's firstborn, was evil in the sight of the Lord, so the Lord took his life. ⁸ Then Judah said to Onan, "Go in to your brother's wife, and perform your duty as a brother-in-law to her, and raise up offspring for your brother." ⁹ Onan knew that the offspring would not be his; so when he went in to his brother's wife, he wasted his seed on the ground in order not to give offspring to his brother. ¹⁰ But what he did was displeasing in the sight of the Lord; so He took his life also. ¹¹ Then Judah said to his daughter-in-law Tamar, "Remain a widow in your father's house until my son Shelah grows up"; for he thought, "I am afraid that he too may die like his brothers." So Tamar went and lived in her father's house. ¹² Now after a considerable time Shua's daughter, the wife of Judah, died; and when the time of mourning was ended, Judah went up to his sheepshearers at Timnah, he and his friend Hirah the Adullamite. ¹³ It was told to Tamar, "Behold, your father-in-law is going up to Timnah to shear his sheep."
¹⁴ So she removed her widow's garments and covered herself with a veil, and wrapped herself, and sat in the gateway of Enaim, which is on the road to Timnah; for she saw that Shelah had grown up, and she had not been given to him as a wife. ¹⁵ When Judah saw her, he thought she was a harlot, for she had covered her face. ¹⁶ So he turned aside to her by the road, and said, "Here now, let me come in to you"; for he did not know that she was his daughter-in-law. And she said, "What will you give me, that you may come

in to me?" ¹⁷ He said, therefore, "I will send you a young goat from the flock." She said, moreover, "Will you give a pledge until you send it?"
¹⁸ He said, "What pledge shall I give you?" And she said, "Your seal and your cord, and your staff that is in your hand." So he gave them to her and went in to her, and she conceived by him. ¹⁹ Then she arose and departed, and removed her veil and put on her widow's garments.
²⁰ When Judah sent the young goat by his friend the Adullamite, to receive the pledge from the woman's hand, he did not find her. ²¹ He asked the men of her place, saying, "Where is the temple prostitute who was by the road at Enaim?" But they said, "There has been no temple prostitute here."
²² So he returned to Judah, and said, "I did not find her; and furthermore, the men of the place said, 'There has been no temple prostitute here.' " ²³ Then Judah said, "Let her keep them, otherwise we will become a laughingstock. After all, I sent this young goat, but you did not find her."
²⁴ Now it was about three months later that Judah was informed, "Your daughter-in-law Tamar has played the harlot, and behold, she is also with child by harlotry." Then Judah said, "Bring her out and let her be burned!"
²⁵ It was while she was being brought out that she sent to her father-in-law, saying, "I am with child by the man to whom these things belong." And she said, "Please examine and see, whose signet ring and cords and staff are these?"
²⁶ Judah recognized them, and said, "She is more righteous than I, inasmuch as I did not give her to my son Shelah." And he did not have relations with her again. ²⁷ It came about at the time she was giving birth, that behold, there were twins in her womb.
²⁸ Moreover, it took place while she was giving birth, one put out a hand, and the midwife took and tied a scarlet

thread on his hand, saying, "This one came out first." ²⁹ But it came about as he drew back his hand, that behold, his brother came out. Then she said, "What a breach you have made for yourself!" So he was named Perez. ³⁰ Afterward his brother came out who had the scarlet thread on his hand; and he was named Zerah.
Genesis 38:1-30 (NASB)

Our culture sees this practice of marrying a deceased brother's wife from a much different perspective, with up-turned noses and uncomfortable feelings. After Judah's first son was killed by the Lord for being evil, marrying Er's wife was a duty based on God's Law that fell into the lap of Er's brother, Onan:

Then Judah said to Onan, "Go in to your brother's wife, and perform your duty as a brother-in-law to her, and raise up offspring for your brother."
Genesis 38:8 (NASB)

The word loosely translated "duty" in the New American Standard Bible is the Hebrew word (יבם) *yabbem*, used here to mean "perform your duty as a brother-in-law." It is used two other times in the Old Testament, as well. Let's look at one of those that explains this issue better:

⁵ "When brothers live together and one of them dies and has no son, the wife of the deceased shall not be married outside the family to a strange man. Her husband's brother shall go in to her and take her to himself as wife and perform the duty of a husband's brother to her. ⁶ "It shall be that the firstborn whom she bears shall assume the name of his dead brother, so that his name will not be blotted out from Israel. ⁷ "But if the man does not desire to take his brother's wife, then his brother's wife

shall go up to the gate to the elders and say, 'My husband's brother refuses to establish a name for his brother in Israel; he is not willing to perform the duty of a husband's brother to me.' [8] "Then the elders of his city shall summon him and speak to him. And if he persists and says, 'I do not desire to take her,' [9] then his brother's wife shall come to him in the sight of the elders, and pull his sandal off his foot and spit in his face; and she shall declare, 'Thus it is done to the man who does not build up his brother's house.' [10] "In Israel his name shall be called, 'The house of him whose sandal is removed.'
Deuteronomy 25:5-10 (NASB)

Again, this seems like a tradition far-removed from what we are accustomed to today. Remember, though, that this is in reference to God's chosen people. God set them apart. In fact, that is what the word "holy" means...to be set apart, not to resemble the rest of the world. God warned the Israelites prophetically that if they married outside of their own tribes that they would seek the gods of their wives. Sadly, that is exactly what occurred, and the children of Israel fell far away from the God of their salvation. This custom is yet another aspect of the Lord's protection from becoming a mirror image of the other nations.

The laws of redemption did not just pertain to people but also to land. Interestingly, the Abrahamic covenant is unconditional in the sense that God said to Abraham:

[1] **Now the Lord said to Abram,
"Go forth from your country,
And from your relatives
And from your father's house,
To the land which I will show you;**

> ² And I will make you a great nation,
> And I will bless you,
> And make your name great;
> And so you shall be a blessing;
> ³ And I will bless those who bless you,
> And the one who curses you I will curse.
> And in you all the families of the earth will be blessed."
> **Genesis 12:1-3 (NASB)**

God's promise to Abraham did not involve performance by Abraham or his relatives for that promise to come to fruition. The Lord then confirmed this promise:

> **The Lord appeared to Abram and said, "To your descendants I will give this land." So he built an altar there to the Lord who had appeared to him.**
> **Genesis 12:7 (NASB)**

Additionally, the Lord confirmed this covenant with Abraham in Genesis 13:14-17, Genesis 15:1-21, Genesis 17:1-21 and Genesis 22:15-18. Also, God continued to confirm this covenant with Isaac in Genesis 25:23 and Genesis 26:23-25, and then also with Jacob in Genesis 28:3-4 and Genesis 28:10-22. Unlike us, God does not break His promises, and fortunately for the descendants of Abraham, the ownership of the land of Israel never would be based upon the behavior of those descendants. But understand that the usage of the land was conditional, upon those descendants following the Lord.

Today, if a man owns a home, he also typically owns the land that the home has been built on. Yet in ancient Israel, God was the owner of the land and had given the children of Israel usage of the land. One of the best descriptions given of the difference between those two involves a father and a teenaged son who receives a new car from the father. The title is in the son's name, but the father tells the son if he gets any tickets that the car is going to sit in the garage for a specified time. That is similar to the covenant that God made with Israel. God gave the children of Israel the land, but there have been periods of time when they lost the usage of that land. Think of the Babylonian captivity that lasted 70 years, and the longest "timeout" God gave the children of Israel occurred when they did not acknowledge Jesus as their Messiah. When the Romans destroyed the Temple in A.D. 70, the Jews departed Israel and were spread out to the four corners of the earth. But in 1948, a miracle occurred. Israel once again became a nation. In 1967, the Jews re-inhabited Jerusalem. The usage of the land had returned, never to be taken away again. How do we know?

**[14] "Also I will restore the captivity of My people Israel,
And they will rebuild the ruined cities and live in them;
They will also plant vineyards and drink their wine,
And make gardens and eat their fruit.
[15] I will also plant them on their land,
And they will not again be rooted out from their land
Which I have given them,"
Says the Lord your God.
Amos 9:14-15 (NASB)**

The laws of land redemption in ancient Israel had to do with that land usage. In terms of land, if a debt was not satisfied, the closest relative could redeem that debt and the collateral land. Remember, the land usage was under God's terms of obedience. When land was sold in ancient Israel, what the buyer received was only the use of the land, not what we would describe as a clear title. And in the Jubilee, which occurred every 50 years, all land returned to the original owner. But without waiting for the year of Jubilee, there were certain conditions under which a kinsman of the seller could satisfy the debt and redeem the land back to the original family. Some biblical scholars have ascertained that these conditions were typically noted on the outside of the scroll defining the transaction. Here's another Old Testament depiction of land redemption:

⁶ And Jeremiah said, "The word of the Lord came to me, saying, ⁷ 'Behold, Hanamel the son of Shallum your uncle is coming to you, saying, "Buy for yourself my field which is at Anathoth, for you have the right of redemption to buy it." ' ⁸ "Then Hanamel my uncle's son came to me in the court of the guard according to the word of the Lord and said to me, 'Buy my field, please, that is at Anathoth, which is in the land of Benjamin; for you have the right of possession and the redemption is yours; buy it for yourself.' Then I knew that this was the word of the Lord. ⁹ "I bought the field which was at Anathoth from Hanamel my uncle's son, and I weighed out the silver for him, seventeen shekels of silver. ¹⁰ "I signed and sealed the deed, and called in witnesses, and weighed out the silver on the scales. ¹¹ "Then I took the deeds of purchase, both the sealed copy containing the terms and conditions and the open copy; ¹² and I gave the deed of purchase to Baruch the son of Neriah, the son of Mahseiah, in the sight of Hanamel my uncle's son and in the sight of the witnesses who signed the deed of purchase, before all the Jews who were sitting in the court of the guard.
Jeremiah 32:6-12 (NASB)

Do not, however, lose sight of the significance redemption has in each of our lives. Because of the sins that we have committed, each of us has a sin debt. We owe God for that debt and under the Law of Moses, the penalty of that sin is death. To satisfy that debt, God gave the children of Israel the ritual of sacrifices, as there can be no forgiveness of sin without the spilling of innocent blood. Even that ritual pointed to Jesus, as He became the Sacrificial Lamb for us all on the cross at Calvary. Because we never could satisfy the debt that we owed to God, Jesus became our Kinsman Redeemer and redeemed our debt for us.

Therefore when Jesus had received the sour wine, He said, "It is finished!" And He bowed His head and gave up His spirit.
John 19:30 (NASB)

The Greek word for "it is finished" in the passage above is *tetelestai* (τετέλεσται), which interestingly, was the same word written on a scroll given to prisoners in that day, who had satisfied their debts to society. Literally, the word means, "paid in full." Why do we as Christians continue to believe that we can add anything to our salvation when Jesus already has done it all for us? Jesus did not say, "It is finished if you are a really good person." Nor did He say, "It is finished as long as you never sin." Our performance has nothing to do with our salvation. That salvation is His gift.

[8] For by grace you have been saved through faith; and that not of yourselves, it is the gift of God;
[9] not as a result of works, so that no one may boast.
[10] For we are His workmanship, created in Christ Jesus for good works, which God prepared beforehand so that we would walk in them.
Ephesians 2:8-10 (NASB)

We have been saved by grace, not by faith. God's Riches At

Christ's Expense. Getting something we do not deserve. But because He loved us first, He wants us to love Him back. How can we do that? Jesus told us:

"If you love Me, you will keep My commandments."
John 14:15 (NASB)

And:

[36] "Teacher, which is the great commandment in the Law?" [37] And He said to him, " 'You shall love the Lord your God with all your heart, and with all your soul, and with all your mind.' [38] "This is the great and foremost commandment. [39] "The second is like it, 'You shall love your neighbor as yourself.' [40] "On these two commandments depend the whole Law and the Prophets."
Matthew 22:36-40 (NASB)

It is just like the words to the song, "They'll know we are Christians by our love!" A "holier than thou" attitude is a big part of the problem!

So as we return to the book of Ruth, we also return to Naomi's thoughts of her daughters-in-law. Remember, Naomi had stated she was not bearing twin sons. Even if she had, it would have been a number of years before those children were born and approached the age of marriage, and stepped into their roles of redeeming Orpah and Ruth. So Naomi again encouraged her daughters-in-law to return to their people, the Moabites, and to find husbands and happy lives. On that second prodding and after a group hug and a girlie cry fest, Orpah chose to return to her people, without thought of changing the spelling of her name slightly and becoming a talk-show hostess. But the young lady in the book's starring role chose to follow Ruth to Israel, and more importantly, Ruth chose to follow Naomi's God!

[16] **But Ruth said, "Do not urge me to leave you or turn back from following you; for where you go, I will go, and where you lodge, I will lodge. Your people shall be my people, and your God, my God.**
[17] **"Where you die, I will die, and there I will be buried. Thus may the Lord do to me, and worse, if anything but death parts you and me."**
[18] **When she saw that she was determined to go with her, she said no more to her.**
Ruth 1:16-18 (NASB)

As Ruth 1 concludes, the two widows arrive in Bethlehem. Though it has been 10 years, the people remember Naomi, who says that she departed full and has returned empty. She asks them not to call her Naomi anymore, but Mara, which means bitterness! By the way, this is the same Hebrew word for Mary, the mother of Jesus, who certainly swallowed a bitter pill at the cross!

DISCUSSION QUESTIONS:

1. For those who are married, what would you do if your spouse and children all died? If you are single, how would you feel if your closest friends all died near the same time?
2. How would this be more difficult if you were living in a foreign country?
3. Has anything ever happened in your life that made you feel like God had abandoned you?

4. Sometimes when our backs are up against the wall, we are surprised, both by the people who show up and by the people we expect to show up who do not. Have you ever experienced this, and if so, when?

5. Who do you feel the most compassion for so far in this story? Who do you most resemble?

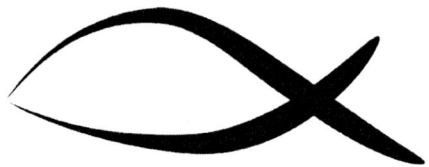

Notes:

Notes:

Chapter 3,
Barley, Wheat and Grapes

With Moab in her past, Ruth finds herself in the field of Boaz, a close relative of Elimelech, at the time of the barley harvest. Take some time reading the details of this story:

[1] **Now Naomi had a kinsman of her husband, a man of great wealth, of the family of Elimelech, whose name was Boaz.**
[2] **And Ruth the Moabitess said to Naomi, "Please let me go to the field and glean among the ears of grain after one in whose sight I may find favor." And she said to her, "Go, my daughter."**
[3] **So she departed and went and gleaned in the field after the reapers; and she happened to come to the portion of the field belonging to Boaz, who was of the family of Elimelech.**
[4] **Now behold, Boaz came from Bethlehem and said to the reapers, "May the Lord be with you." And they said to him, "May the Lord bless you."**
[5] **Then Boaz said to his servant who was in charge of the reapers, "Whose young woman is this?"**

⁶ The servant in charge of the reapers replied, "She is the young Moabite woman who returned with Naomi from the land of Moab. ⁷ "And she said, 'Please let me glean and gather after the reapers among the sheaves.' Thus she came and has remained from the morning until now; she has been sitting in the house for a little while." ⁸ Then Boaz said to Ruth, "Listen carefully, my daughter. Do not go to glean in another field; furthermore, do not go on from this one, but stay here with my maids.
⁹ "Let your eyes be on the field which they reap, and go after them. Indeed, I have commanded the servants not to touch you. When you are thirsty, go to the water jars and drink from what the servants draw." ¹⁰ Then she fell on her face, bowing to the ground and said to him, "Why have I found favor in your sight that you should take notice of me, since I am a foreigner?"
¹¹ Boaz replied to her, "All that you have done for your mother-in-law after the death of your husband has been fully reported to me, and how you left your father and your mother and the land of your birth, and came to a people that you did not previously know. ¹² "May the Lord reward your work, and your wages be full from the Lord, the God of Israel, under whose wings you have come to seek refuge."
¹³ Then she said, "I have found favor in your sight, my lord, for you have comforted me and indeed have spoken kindly to your maidservant, though I am not like one of your maidservants."
¹⁴ At mealtime Boaz said to her, "Come here, that you may eat of the bread and dip your piece of bread in the vinegar." So she sat beside the reapers; and he served her roasted grain, and she ate and was satisfied and had some left.
¹⁵ When she rose to glean, Boaz commanded his servants, saying, "Let her glean even among the sheaves, and do not insult her. ¹⁶ "Also you shall purposely pull out for

her some grain from the bundles and leave it that she may glean, and do not rebuke her." [17] So she gleaned in the field until evening. Then she beat out what she had gleaned, and it was about an ephah of barley. [18] She took it up and went into the city, and her mother-in-law saw what she had gleaned. She also took it out and gave Naomi what she had left after she was satisfied.

[19] Her mother-in-law then said to her, "Where did you glean today and where did you work? May he who took notice of you be blessed." So she told her mother-in-law with whom she had worked and said, "The name of the man with whom I worked today is Boaz."

[20] Naomi said to her daughter-in-law, "May he be blessed of the Lord who has not withdrawn his kindness to the living and to the dead." Again Naomi said to her, "The man is our relative, he is one of our closest relatives."

[21] Then Ruth the Moabitess said, "Furthermore, he said to me, 'You should stay close to my servants until they have finished all my harvest.' " [22] Naomi said to Ruth her daughter-in-law, "It is good, my daughter, that you go out with his maids, so that others do not fall upon you in another field." [23] So she stayed close by the maids of Boaz in order to glean until the end of the barley harvest and the wheat harvest. And she lived with her mother-in-law.
Ruth 2:1-23 (NASB)

Chapter 2 involves the ancient practice of gleaning, also called scrounging. In biblical times, gleaning was collecting the crops remaining after the harvest. Some people look at it as a biblical version of the welfare system, but notice that this was not an example of the wealthy handing food or money to the impoverished. Instead, it was the "haves" giving the "have-nots" the ability to work for their sustenance. In Yosemite National Park, the rangers hand out hefty fines when campers leave food out at a campsite. Unfortunately, the bears get used to our leftovers, and instead of foraging for their food naturally, once they discover this much easier approach, begin to count on our sloppy seconds. Each campsite contains a bear locker, and as soon as the cooking is finished, the food must be stored in that safe location. Bears also have broken into cars when food is stored there! The rangers must kill the bears that continue to glean the food in campsites, but it is not the bears' fault, but the fault of the people. In the same way, we have to be cautious doing for others what they need to do for themselves, but the Bible also teaches for us to feed the hungry. Giving those hungry a way to feed themselves is even a better solution, but is not always possible. We need to treat each case individually. Gleaning accomplishes that very well, and is one of the laws given by God numerous times in the Old Testament:

[17] **"You shall not pervert the justice due an alien or an orphan, nor take a widow's garment in pledge.** [18] **"But you shall remember that you were a slave in Egypt, and that the Lord your God redeemed you from there; therefore I am commanding you to do this thing.**
[19] **"When you reap your harvest in your field and have forgotten a sheaf in the field, you shall not go back to get it; it shall be for the alien, for the orphan, and for the widow, in order that the Lord your God may bless you in all the work of your hands.** [20] **"When you beat your olive tree, you shall not go over the boughs again; it shall be for the alien, for the orphan, and for the widow.**
[21] **"When you gather the grapes of your vineyard, you shall not go over it again; it shall be for the alien, for the orphan, and for the widow.** [22] **"You shall remember that you were a slave in the land of Egypt; therefore I am commanding you**

**to do this thing.
Deuteronomy 24:17-22 (NASB)**

Often in the Old Testament, God reminds the children of Israel to treat aliens well. God knew they certainly would understand what it felt like to be strangers in a strange land. He often places believers into similar situations that He has delivered us from, for in those places, we have true compassion. Compassion is often defined as feeling someone else's pain, and the easiest way to feel that pain is through memory rather than through trying to understand pain we never have experienced. Think of the Native American adage, "Never criticize a man until you have walked in his moccasins." When we read about God saving the children of Israel from Pharaoh's advancing soldiers by parting the Red Sea, and then days later, those same people created and worshipped a golden calf, most of us cannot fathom the depth of that idiocy. But with a little circumspection, all of us can find times in our own lives when the Lord showed His miraculous hand, but days later, we also doubted Him! These verses are not describing sinful Jews; they are describing us!

These strangers in strange lands can be different in language, appearance and culture. John Donne reminded us that, "No man is an island," and we know that it is difficult to not feel connected. Naomi certainly felt disconnected in the land of Moab. Notice the categories of people used as examples in the biblical law of gleaning – aliens, widows and orphans. In a way, Naomi could be counted in each category. She obviously was an alien, in the land of Moab instead of in her homeland of Israel. Additionally, Naomi's husband was deceased, making her a widow. Finally, her parents were no longer alive, though we think of an orphan as a child without parents, rather than an adult without parents. But Naomi also felt abandoned by her heavenly Father. As this story continues, though, we can see that while she might have felt abandoned by God, He was completely in charge of her life!

The worst kind of orphan on this earth is the child of God who is not walking with God. No pain is greater, for once we walk in the light, darkness is overwhelming. God allows us to choose pain at times in our lives, for when we return to Him, our trust and faith in Him has grown much stronger. How alone must Naomi have felt in Moab after her husband and two sons both died! Now, though, the tables have turned and Ruth is in that role of alien in Israel.

When I was riding on a train from San Diego to Los Angeles soon after moving to California, the conductor stopped the train after many riding the train began to yell, "There's an alien on the train! There's an alien on the train." This recent-California resident had different thoughts of the word "alien," thinking those crazy Californians must have seen an Unidentified Flying Object land on top of the train! But after the train stopped, an unidentified Hispanic man ran from the train, as he had been riding on top to avoid the immigration checkpoint. Two themes seemed apparent after that experience. First, everything is not as it appears. Second, we as Christians are supposed to feel like aliens on this earth! Though God created this world for us, we know that He has given Satan dominion over this earth for now. In the Garden of Eden, Adam and Eve were home, but ever since sin entered the world, we can look ahead to the world without sin as our true home. As believers, we should feel like strangers in a strange land! Jesus told His disciples that they were to be in the world, but not of the world.

[18] "If the world hates you, you know that it has hated Me before it hated you. [19] "If you were of the world, the world would love its own; but because you are not of the world, but I chose you out of the world, because of this the world hates you. [20] "Remember the word that I said to you, 'A slave is not greater than his master.' If they persecuted Me, they will also persecute you; if they kept My word, they will keep yours also.
John 15:18-20 (NASB)

Being in the world yet not of the world involves a little fence straddling, and men can testify that standing with one foot on the ground on each side of that fence is not a very comfortable place. Instead of resembling the people of this world who surround us, we are to resemble our Savior. Paul added to that sentiment when he said,

And do not be conformed to this world, but be transformed by the renewing of your mind, so that you may prove what the will of God is, that which is good and acceptable and perfect.
Romans 12:2 (NASB)

Christians certainly are not in the majority on this earth. When faced with the concept that majority rules, that majority is following Satan, rather than God, as God has given him temporary dominion over this broken world. Let's return to another verse about gleaning to assemble this concept:

When you reap the harvest of your land, moreover, you shall not reap to the very corners of your field nor gather the gleaning of your harvest; you are to leave them for the needy and the alien. I am the Lord your God.' "
Leviticus 23:22 (NASB)

These could have looked like "crop circles," for if the corners remained, the harvested area could be a circle in the middle! Interestingly, God often focuses on a remnant. In this story, a remnant of the crops supplied the needs for a remnant of the people. God provided for Ruth and Naomi just as He provides for any remnant of His believers. Revelation points to a time when a remnant of 144,000, 12,000 men from each of the 12 tribes, will evangelize during the Great Tribulation. They will be sealed and protected by the Holy Spirit. Here is what Paul said about another remnant.

¹ I say then, God has not rejected His people, has He? May it never be! For I too am an Israelite, a descendant of Abraham, of the tribe of Benjamin. ² God has not rejected His people whom He foreknew. Or do you not know what the Scripture says in the passage about Elijah, how he pleads with God against Israel? ³ "Lord, they have killed Your prophets, they have torn down Your altars, and I alone am left, and they are seeking my life."
⁴ But what is the divine response to him? "I have kept for Myself seven thousand men who have not bowed the knee to Baal." ⁵ In the same way then, there has also come to be at the present time a remnant according to God's gracious choice.
Romans 11:1-5 (NASB)

It seems that in every generation there is a remnant set aside by God and for God. Just as God had Gideon pare down his army from 32,000 to 300 In Judges 7, just as God had David conquer the giant Goliath armed with five, smooth stones and a sling, just as God sent His chosen people into the chosen land of Israel, though there were giants in the Land, He goes before each of us. In the same manner, God prepared the way for Naomi, who felt abandoned by Him, and prepared the way for

Ruth.

So as Chapter 2 of Ruth begins, we meet Boaz, the near relative of Elimelech, Naomi's deceased husband. Boaz appears to be a wealthy landowner, employing many, especially in the time of the barley harvest. We also see that Boaz wishes the Lord's blessing on his workers. Boaz then takes notice of this unknown, young woman in his field, and asks his unnamed servant, head of the reapers, about her.

⁵ Then Boaz said to his servant who was in charge of the reapers, "Whose young woman is this?"
⁶ The servant in charge of the reapers replied, "She is the young Moabite woman who returned with Naomi from the land of Moab.
⁷ "And she said, 'Please let me glean and gather after the reapers among the sheaves.' Thus she came and has remained from the morning until now; she has been sitting in the house for a little while."
⁸ Then Boaz said to Ruth, "Listen carefully, my daughter. Do not go to glean in another field; furthermore, do not go on from this one, but stay here with my maids.
Ruth 2:5-8 (NASB)

Not only was Boaz a godly man, but also we see that Ruth was truly seeking the God of her mother-in-law Naomi. Boaz understood the law of gleaning, but when Ruth questioned him why he was being so good to her, Boaz told her that he was aware of the love she was showing to her mother-in-law. He saw that she had left her land, her people, her language and her gods. Additionally, it was not just lip service from Ruth, but she had put her love into action, working from morning to night to supply the bread for herself and Naomi, during this barley harvest. Boaz looked at Ruth, and regardless of what he saw on the outside, he liked what he saw on the inside!

In biblical times, the barley harvest occurred in the spring. On our calendars, that is March or April, but on the Hebrew calendar, it was the time of Passover. Passover occurs along with the first full moon after the first day of spring, but before this day was determined mathematically, it was the first full moon after the barley harvest. In the seven Feasts of Moses discussed thoroughly in the Old Testament, we know that three of those occur in the spring, three in the fall and one between. The three spring feasts are the Feast of Unleavened Bread, the Feast of Passover and the Feast of Firstfruits.

[4] 'These are the appointed times of the Lord, holy convocations which you shall proclaim at the times appointed for them. [5] 'In the first month, on the fourteenth day of the month at twilight is the Lord's Passover. [6] 'Then on the fifteenth day of the same month there is the Feast of Unleavened Bread to the Lord; for seven days you shall eat unleavened bread.
[7] 'On the first day you shall have a holy convocation; you shall not do any laborious work. [8] 'But for seven days you shall present an offering by fire to the Lord. On the seventh day is a holy convocation; you shall not do any laborious work.' "
[9] Then the Lord spoke to Moses, saying,
[10] "Speak to the sons of Israel and say to them, 'When you enter the land which I am going to give to you and reap its harvest, then you shall bring in the sheaf of the first fruits of your harvest to the priest. [11] 'He shall wave the sheaf before the Lord for you to be accepted; on the day after the sabbath the priest shall wave it.
[12] 'Now on the day when you wave the sheaf, you shall offer a male lamb one year old without defect for a burnt

offering to the Lord. [13] 'Its grain offering shall then be two-tenths of an ephah of fine flour mixed with oil, an offering by fire to the Lord for a soothing aroma, with its drink offering, a fourth of a hin of wine.
Leviticus 23:4-13 (NASB)

The sheaf discussed in verses 11-12 above was barley, for this was the firstfruit of the harvest. The LORD was not to be given what was left over. Instead, the offering to Him came at the beginning of the harvest. This practice involves faith! Jesus testified of the widow who gave out of her poverty, rather than the others who gave out of their abundance (Luke 21). While the barley harvest occurred at Passover, the wheat harvest occurred at Pentecost. Even before that first Passover night, with the Jews enslaved to Pharaoh and Egypt, God judged Egypt with hail, the seventh plague.

[28] "Make supplication to the Lord, for there has been enough of God's thunder and hail; and I will let you go, and you shall stay no longer." [29] Moses said to him, "As soon as I go out of the city, I will spread out my hands to the Lord; the thunder will cease and there will be hail no longer, that you may know that the earth is the Lord's.
[30] "But as for you and your servants, I know that you do not yet fear the Lord God." [31] (Now the flax and the barley were ruined, for the barley was in the ear and the flax was in bud. [32] But the wheat and the spelt were not ruined, for they ripen late.)
Exodus 9:28-32 (NASB)

The flax and the barley were ruined by this hailstorm, but the wheat was unaffected, as it had not grown yet! Part of God's judgment on Egypt involved this barley harvest, and it is easy to see the plagues in Egypt as similar occurrences in the Great

Tribulation, with His wrath multiplied in the latter days.

And I heard something like a voice in the center of the four living creatures saying, "A quart of wheat for a denarius, and three quarts of barley for a denarius; and do not damage the oil and the wine."
Revelation 6:6 (NASB)

A denarius was silver, Roman coin, and was the equivalent of a day's wage for the typical worker in biblical times. This prophesied famine will be a time when a man's wages will buy him one meal of wheat or three meals of barley. Many believe that the reference to oil and wine reveal that there will be no money remaining for those luxuries. Others believe that this reference to luxury items describes a time when the poor will be greatly affected, but the wealthy will be unaffected. Barley seems to be very significant in the Bible. Let's look at some of those other occurrences:

[42] Now a man came from Baal-shalishah, and brought the man of God bread of the first fruits, twenty loaves of barley and fresh ears of grain in his sack. And he said, "Give them to the people that they may eat."
[43] His attendant said, "What, will I set this before a hundred men?" But he said, "Give them to the people that they may eat, for thus says the Lord, 'They shall eat and have some left over.'" [44] So he set it before them, and they ate and had some left over, according to the word of the Lord.
2 Kings 4:42-44 (NASB)

Elisha, through God's miracle, abundantly fed the sons of the prophets. Though there was a small amount of food, the men were satiated with food remaining. Even the food has a remnant when God is the provider. A similar miracle continues in the New Testament:

⁵ Therefore Jesus, lifting up His eyes and seeing that a large crowd was coming to Him, said to Philip, "Where are we to buy bread, so that these may eat?"
⁶ This He was saying to test him, for He Himself knew what He was intending to do.
⁷ Philip answered Him, "Two hundred denarii worth of bread is not sufficient for them, for everyone to receive a little."
⁸ One of His disciples, Andrew, Simon Peter's brother, said to Him,
⁹ "There is a lad here who has five barley loaves and two fish, but what are these for so many people?"
¹⁰ Jesus said, "Have the people sit down." Now there was much grass in the place. So the men sat down, in number about five thousand.
¹¹ Jesus then took the loaves, and having given thanks, He distributed to those who were seated; likewise also of the fish as much as they wanted.
¹² When they were filled, He said to His disciples, "Gather up the leftover fragments so that nothing will be lost."
John 6:5-12 (NASB)

It seems that God often uses barley to feed His people miraculously! Some Bible scholars point out that there are three different harvests discussed in the Bible and each of those pertain to the harvest of a different group of people. The barley and wheat harvests seem to apply to believers, while the grape harvest applies to the judgment of unbelievers. Let's look at the wheat harvest through the words of Jesus:

²⁴ **Jesus presented another parable to them, saying, "The kingdom of heaven may be compared to a man who sowed**

good seed in his field. [25] "But while his men were sleeping, his enemy came and sowed tares among the wheat, and went away. [26] "But when the wheat sprouted and bore grain, then the tares became evident also.
[27] "The slaves of the landowner came and said to him, 'Sir, did you not sow good seed in your field? How then does it have tares?' [28] "And he said to them, 'An enemy has done this!' The slaves said to him, 'Do you want us, then, to go and gather them up?' [29] "But he said, 'No; for while you are gathering up the tares, you may uproot the wheat with them.
[30] 'Allow both to grow together until the harvest; and in the time of the harvest I will say to the reapers, "First gather up the tares and bind them in bundles to burn them up; but gather the wheat into my barn."'"
Matthew 13:24-30 (NASB)

As believers, we are the wheat, with seeds planted by the Lord. We are growing alongside the tares, the unbelievers in this world. Rather than uprooting all of the tares, and disturbing the growth of the wheat, God has chosen to let the two grow simultaneously. When it is time for the harvest, He will separate the two. This is the process of winnowing that will be even more apparent in the third chapter of Ruth. The grape harvest is another category, entirely, with much symbolism in the Old Testament drawing a correlation between Israel and the grapevine. Psalm 80 makes this evident, by stating,

[8] **You removed a vine from Egypt;**
You drove out the nations and planted it.
[9] **You cleared the ground before it,**
And it took deep root and filled the land.
Psalm 80:8-9 (NASB)

That vine removed from Egypt was Israel, with its children enslaved to Pharaoh before the events of that first Passover night. God prepared the land for His chosen people, and certainly, the children of Israel filled the land. This correlation becomes more obvious in the words of the prophet Isaiah:

> [1] **Let me sing now for my well-beloved**
> **A song of my beloved concerning His vineyard.**
> **My well-beloved had a vineyard on a fertile hill.**
> [2] **He dug it all around, removed its stones,**
> **And planted it with the choicest vine.**
> **And He built a tower in the middle of it**
> **And also hewed out a wine vat in it;**
> **Then He expected it to produce good grapes,**
> **But it produced only worthless ones.**
> [3] **"And now, O inhabitants of Jerusalem and men of Judah,**
> **Judge between My vineyard and Me.**
> [4] **"What more was there to do for My vineyard that I have not done in it?**
> **Why, when I expected it to produce good grapes did it produce worthless ones?**
> [5] **"So now let Me tell you what I am going to do to My vineyard:**
> **I will remove its hedge and it will be consumed;**
> **I will break down its wall and it will become trampled ground.**
> **Isaiah 5:1-5 (NASB)**

Differentiation between good grapes and wild grapes has nothing to do with the role of the Vinedresser, who is God the Father. He did everything to cultivate ALL good grapes, but these personified grapes have free will along with the ability to choose between following the Vinedresser or not following the Vinedresser. His final judgment will occur with the final battle,

Armageddon. The Hebrew word for mountain is *har*, and this battle will occur in the Jezreel (Jehoshaphat) Valley, just below Mount Megiddo. *Har-Megiddo* = Armageddon. According to the Book of Revelation, this will be a veritable bloodbath.

And the wine press was trodden outside the city, and blood came out from the wine press, up to the horses' bridles, for a distance of two hundred miles.
Revelation 14:20 (NASB)

That is so much blood that it is hard to imagine it is not hyperbole. Yet this battle involves all nations on the earth, and sadly, the river of blood described could be just as described. Other verses from the Old Testament also speak prophetically of God's judgment on mankind in reference to the winepress along with the final grape harvest.

[1] Who is this who comes from Edom,
With garments of glowing colors from Bozrah,
This One who is majestic in His apparel,
Marching in the greatness of His strength?
"It is I who speak in righteousness, mighty to save."
[2] Why is Your apparel red,
And Your garments like the one who treads in the wine press?
[3] "I have trodden the wine trough alone,
And from the peoples there was no man with Me.
I also trod them in My anger
And trampled them in My wrath;
And their lifeblood is sprinkled on My garments,
And I stained all My raiment.
Isaiah 63:1-3 (NASB)

¹² Let the nations be aroused
And come up to the valley of Jehoshaphat,
For there I will sit to judge
All the surrounding nations.
¹³ Put in the sickle, for the harvest is ripe.
Come, tread, for the wine press is full;
The vats overflow, for their wickedness is great.
¹⁴ Multitudes, multitudes in the valley of decision!
For the day of the Lord is near in the valley of decision.
Joel 3:12-14 (NASB)

Most of us are familiar with the chorus of "Glory, Glory, Hallelujah," in Julia Ward Howe's song "The Battle Hymn of the Republic," but this generation seems to have difficulty remembering the verse that points to this future judgment,

"Mine eyes have seen the glory of the coming of the LORD,
He has trampled out the vintage where the grapes of wrath are stored.
He hath loosed the fateful lightning of His terrible swift sword.
His truth is marching on."

In the agrarian economy of the Bible, it is easy to see why God used so many harvest-oriented symbols to explain our relationships with Him. He plants the seeds. He waters the seeds. He clears the weeds. And most importantly, He harvests those seeds, once they have grown to become what was intended when they were planted!

DISCUSSION QUESTIONS:

1. Do you think it is a coincidence that both Elisha and Jesus fed multitudes miraculously with barley?

2. What are some of the common usages of barley today? Was barley used similarly in biblical times?
3. Other than the timing of the harvest, what are some of the differences between barley and wheat?
4. What is the meaning of the Feast of Firstfruits? Even if we are not farmers, how can we give our Firstfruits to the LORD today? How is this connected with faith?
5. Name some other verses in the Bible that have to do with the harvest.

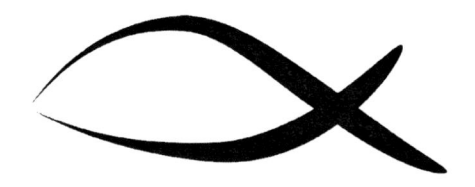

Notes:

Notes:

Chapter 4,
Strangers in a Strange Land

With all this information as background to the events of Ruth 2, let's return to the fields of Boaz in Bethlehem. Our quaint story is about to become a romance, as the cast of characters seems to be dwindling, to this landowner and the impoverished daughter-in-law of Naomi, the Moabitess named Ruth. In Chapter 2, Boaz reveals so much about his character. Remember, "character" is described as who we are when no one else is looking. Paul reminds us in Ephesians 4:1 to walk worthy of God's calling. "Worthy" is the Greek word *axios*, which refer to the scales used in the Greek marketplace. In that economy based on weight, a vendor would place the item for sale on one side of the scale and the currency on the other side of the scale. When in balance, the trade was a good one. God desires for us to be in balance, as well. Our walk with Him should be the same on a Sunday at church and in our business dealings during the week. Instead of lying, cheating and stealing to get ahead, God desires for us to act with His moral standards in all situations. If an enemy spreads vicious lies that cause pain, God will defend His honor, for when we have been purchased with His blood, that honor is no longer ours!

When we look at the character of Boaz in this chapter, we see the following:

Character trait Of Boaz	Bible Verse
Man of great wealth	Ruth 2:1
Close relative of Elimelech	Ruth 2:1
From Bethlehem	Ruth 2:3
Worships God	Ruth 2:4
Observant	Ruth 2:11
Comforter	Ruth 2:13
Feeds the hungry	Ruth 2:14
Servant	Ruth 2:14
Protector	Ruth 2:15
Provider	Ruth 2:16

As the chapter begins, we see that Boaz is a man of great wealth, from the family of Elimelech, and his land is located in Bethlehem. Bethlehem is an important location in the Bible as we remember it as the birthplace of Jesus. In Hebrew, Bethlehem means "house of bread." Verse 4 reveals to us how Boaz feels about the God of Israel. He did not just believe silently, but spoke of God to his workers, and we also should note that his workers were comfortable in speaking about God to Boaz, as well. Certainly, his workers and neighbors recognized Boaz as a man of God. Boaz discusses Ruth with his servant, who was in charge of the reapers, and the same man introduced Boaz to Ruth. Verse 11 shows us how observant Boaz is, as nothing has gotten past him concerning

Ruth. Boaz knows who she is, where she came from, and what she left in Moab, Most importantly, he notices that she is seeking God and reveals that heart change in this amazing compassion for her mother-in-law Naomi. In verse 14, Boaz feeds Ruth, knowing she is hungry from her full day of work along with a rough patch in her life. The same verse highlights that he served her, so this wealthy man is also a servant! In verse 15, Boaz offers to protect Ruth, and finally, in verse 16, he offers provision for her, offering to be her provider of sorts.

Finally, let's look at our leading lady, Ruth, and find out some of her character traits. We already know that she is a young widow, but let's see the personality or character traits included in this chapter:

Verse 2 reminds us that she is from the land of Moab; in verse 2 we also see that she is poor (we have no idea if that is something she has been accustomed to all her life, but we know that is her station in life presently); in verse 7, we see she is a hard worker; in verse 8, she appears to be a very good listener; in verse 10, she is thankful; in verse 12, we see Ruth as a seeker of God; in verse 14, she is hungry; and in verse 18, we see that she shares with Naomi, and has become her provider.

Character trait of Ruth	Bible Verse
From Moab	Ruth 2:2
Poor	Ruth 2:2
Hard worker	Ruth 2:7
Good listener	Ruth 2:8
Thankful	Ruth 2:10
Compassionate	Ruth 2:11
Seeker of God	Ruth 2:12

Character trait of Ruth	Bible Verse
Hungry	Ruth 2:14
Sharer	Ruth 2:18
Provider	Ruth 2:18

We do not know how long Boaz had been seeking the LORD, but we know that Ruth's conversion had occurred recently. Certainly, she had heard about the God of the children of Israel from her husband, but in the journey to Israel, it is likely that Ruth heard much more from Naomi. Pressed with hardships from every angle, though, Ruth is turning to God and honoring Him in all of her actions. Later, God made this promise to the children of Israel:

**"Therefore the LORD God of Israel declares, 'I did indeed say that your house and the house of your father should walk before Me forever'; but now the LORD declares, 'Far be it from Me—for those who honor Me I will honor, and those who despise Me will be lightly esteemed.
1 Samuel 2:30 (NASB)**

In the New Testament, Jesus put it this way:

**"If anyone serves Me, he must follow Me; and where I am, there My servant will be also; if anyone serves Me, the Father will honor him.
John 12:26 (NASB)**

As this wonderful book of the Old Testament continues, we

will see God complete that promise in the lives of these believers!

DISCUSSION QUESTIONS:

1. Boaz is an amazing man. Is there anyone in your life who reminds you of Boaz? Do you know anyone who reminds you of Ruth?
2. What is the best way to address poverty and homelessness—individually, through our churches or through our government?
3. Is it easier to seek the LORD when times are difficult or when times are great? What does this tell us about Boaz?
4. Do you think Boaz treated all the poor women gleaning in his fields the same way he treated Ruth? Why or why not?
5. Share some examples of God's provision when you were in difficult times. How was your faith affected? Did you fall back into doubt after that time?

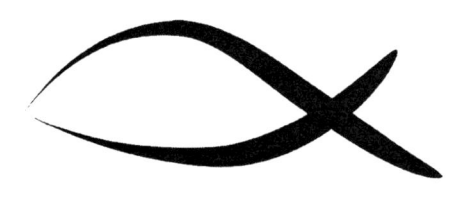

Notes:

Chapter 5,
There is a Redeemer!

Much has happened since Ruth and Naomi ventured from Moab to Bethlehem. Hungry, tired and still without a breadwinner, Ruth goes to work in a "random" field, which turns out to be that of a close relative of Naomi's deceased husband, Elimelech. That close relative is the wealthy landowner Boaz, who takes a shining to Ruth after being introduced by a servant of Boaz. Boaz instructs Ruth to continue to glean in the land through both the barley harvest and the wheat harvest, the time period from Passover to Pentecost. In addition, he feeds Ruth. She goes home with food in belly and food in hand, with plenty remaining for Naomi, as well. Chapter 2 ends with the two widows discussing Boaz, and that conversation continues as Chapter 3 begins:

[1] **Then Naomi her mother-in-law said to her, "My daughter, shall I not seek security for you, that it may be well with you?** [2] **"Now is not Boaz our kinsman, with whose maids**

you were? Behold, he winnows barley at the threshing floor tonight.

³ "Wash yourself therefore, and anoint yourself and put on your best clothes, and go down to the threshing floor; but do not make yourself known to the man until he has finished eating and drinking.

⁴ "It shall be when he lies down, that you shall notice the place where he lies, and you shall go and uncover his feet and lie down; then he will tell you what you shall do." ⁵ She said to her, "All that you say I will do."

⁶ So she went down to the threshing floor and did according to all that her mother-in-law had commanded her. ⁷ When Boaz had eaten and drunk and his heart was merry, he went to lie down at the end of the heap of grain; and she came secretly, and uncovered his feet and lay down.

⁸ It happened in the middle of the night that the man was startled and bent forward; and behold, a woman was lying at his feet.

⁹ He said, "Who are you?" And she answered, "I am Ruth your maid. So spread your covering over your maid, for you are a close relative." ¹⁰ Then he said, "May you be blessed of the Lord, my daughter. You have shown your last kindness to be better than the first by not going after young men, whether poor or rich.

¹¹ "Now, my daughter, do not fear. I will do for you whatever you ask, for all my people in the city know that you are a woman of excellence. ¹² "Now it is true I am a close relative; however, there is a relative closer than I.

¹³ "Remain this night, and when morning comes, if he will redeem you, good; let him redeem you. But if he does not wish to redeem you, then I will redeem you, as the Lord lives. Lie down until morning." ¹⁴ So she lay at his feet until morning and rose before one could recognize another; and he said, "Let it not be known that the woman came to the

threshing floor."
¹⁵ Again he said, "Give me the cloak that is on you and hold it." So she held it, and he measured six measures of barley and laid it on her. Then she went into the city.
¹⁶ When she came to her mother-in-law, she said, "How did it go, my daughter?" And she told her all that the man had done for her. ¹⁷ She said, "These six measures of barley he gave to me, for he said, 'Do not go to your mother-in-law empty-handed.' " ¹⁸ Then she said, "Wait, my daughter, until you know how the matter turns out; for the man will not rest until he has settled it today."
Ruth 3:1-18 (NASB)

Ruth's day has been a long one already, but with Naomi's instructions, that day is just beginning. Being Jewish, Naomi understands the legal principles of a Levirate marriage, which we discussed extensively in Chapter 2. The Latin word *levir* means "husband's brother," and this process was one of the ways that God's Law protected the Jewish nation from worshipping other gods. Remember what occurred when Judah's son Er died. His brother Onan was supposed to take his brother Er's place and provide children for Er's wife, Tamar. But Onan acted selfishly and the LORD took his life, as well. This was not a suggestion from the LORD, but a Law! By the Law of Levirate marriage, Naomi is encouraging her daughter-in-law to pursue Boaz for security. Though Ruth has toiled all day in the field harvesting, Naomi encourages her to clean up and change clothes. Ruth 3:3 points to three symbolic gestures that Ruth made that night in preparation. She washed, symbolic of purification from her idolatrous past, worshipping foreign gods. Also, she anointed herself, symbolic of her
acceptance of the covenant of the *Torah*. Finally, she put on new dressing. This was likely a new Sabbath garment, symbolizing observation of the Law of Moses. All of these are

significant, as they demonstrate that Ruth truly has converted to Judaism, and is now seeking the One True God. Instead of sleeping, Ruth is going fishing...for a husband, and she has a particular man in mind.

For this is the night when Boaz will be winnowing the barley from the day's harvest. Winnowing occurred at a certain place on the threshing floor, and these locations always were placed precisely where there would be a prevailing wind. The workers tossed what had been harvested into the air, and separation occurred. The grain fell to the ground, while the lighter chaff blew downwind. When completed, the process would yield grain, barley in this case, and a separate pile of chaff, which was burned as trash. In an agrarian economy, this was a most festive night, and though the workers were tired, it was a great night of celebration. Part involved the culmination of much labor, but in ancient Israel, another aspect involved thanks to the LORD, who had watered the crops and protected them. God had promised that if the children of Israel followed His laws, He would not bring famine.

Naomi then gives Ruth a strange instruction about uncovering the feet of Boaz. Some people misinterpret this passage, but we see other verses where the Bible seems to speak in euphemisms. Let's look at one of those:

[1]And it came to pass, when Saul was returned from following the Philistines, that it was told him, saying, Behold, David is in the wilderness of En-gedi. [2] Then Saul took three thousand chosen men out of all Israel, and went to seek David and his men upon the rocks of the wild goats. [3] And he came to the sheepcotes by the way, where was a cave; and Saul went in to cover his feet: and David and his men remained in the sides of the cave. [4] And the men of

David said unto him, Behold the day of which the Lord said unto thee, Behold, I will deliver thine enemy into thine hand, that thou mayest do to him as it shall seem good unto thee. Then David arose, and cut off the skirt of Saul's robe privily.
1 Samuel 24:1-4 (King James Version)

In the King James Version quoted above, we see that King Saul was in a cave of En-gedi and went in to "cover his feet." This was not because the King's feet had grown cold. Instead, as the NASB puts it, King Saul went in to relieve himself. The outer garment for a man of standing was called a *simlah*, and the hem of that garment also carried his standing or rank, in much the same way that rank is displayed on the shoulder board of a military man. In this case, David could have killed King Saul, who at that moment was seeking David's life. Instead, David cut off a piece of the hem of the King's garment. When the two were no longer alone, David displayed the piece of that garment, and apologized to King Saul for cutting it. That action showed King Saul that David could have killed him if David had chosen, for it took a knife to cut the garment and King Saul had no idea David had been with him. It also revealed David's heart. We also see similar terminology in Genesis 9:22 when Noah was "uncovered" in his tent and Ham saw the nakedness of his father. When Noah awoke, knowing what Ham had done, he cursed Ham's son Canaan. As we return to the statement Naomi makes to Ruth, to uncover the feet of Boaz, we do not need to apply this same euphemism.

The same significance does continue, though, with the hem of the *simlah* of Boaz. Naomi instructs Ruth to wait until Boaz has finished eating and drinking. When he lies down, Ruth is to lie at his feet and uncover those feet, and Naomi tells Ruth that Boaz will decide what happens next. Our culture would expect Boaz to take off Ruth's clothes or the rest of his, but that is not what is going on here. Boaz is a godly man who believes in and keeps God's commandments. Ruth follows the instructions of her mother-in-law, and is so quiet that Boaz continues to sleep. Yet in the middle of the night, he awakens:

⁸ It happened in the middle of the night that the man was startled and bent forward; and behold, a woman was lying at his feet.
⁹ He said, "Who are you?" And she answered, "I am Ruth your maid. So spread your covering over your maid, for you are a close relative."
Ruth 3:8-9 (NASB)

When Boaz asks this maiden to identify herself, Ruth identifies herself, and then asks for him to spread his covering over her. Ruth would like that title or standing that once covered only Boaz to cover her as well. She is asking for him to become her kinsman redeemer. In Hebrew, a kinsman redeemer was a *goel*. (לאג) Notice that Boaz does not offer this service, but Ruth requests it. It seems that both Boaz and Ruth had experienced that feeling of love-at-first-sight earlier in the day, but it is more likely that it was much more than physical attraction. Boaz had exhibited such godly attributes, and Ruth was in dire straits. But if Boaz thought she was beautiful in her work clothes, this night she is dressed up and anointed! And lest we forget, his heart was merry in celebration of the harvest.

And wine which makes man's heart glad,
So that he may make his face glisten with oil,
And food which sustains man's heart.
Psalm 104:15 (NASB)

Boaz sounds ecstatic when he speaks of the fact that Ruth could have chosen a younger man, whether rich or poor. Once again, he noticed Ruth's compassion in taking care of Naomi, and now sees that compassionate heart continue in choosing him, as he is certainly not a young man if we understand this descriptive speech. Boaz offers her a blessing from the LORD and acknowledges that he would be happy to act in the role of the *goel*, or kinsman redeemer. In order to fulfill the duties of a Levirate marriage, the *goel* needed to be a kinsman (we know that Boaz was a close relative of Elimelech, the father-in-law of Ruth, but this requirement more specifically was to be a blood relative); he needed to be willing (Boaz might be the most willing man in the history of men); he also needed to be able. This ability could involve having the resources to pay the price, or even being unmarried. Interestingly, this third requirement could actually be problematic for Boaz, but not wanting to lead Ruth on, he instantly tells her that there actually is another closer kinsman redeemer. Boaz encourages Ruth to sleep, and that they will figure it all out in the morning. If the closer relative is willing and able, he can redeem Ruth, but if not, Boaz will gladly perform that duty.

These requirements were scriptural, based on the Law of God. Let's look at some of those:

[23] **'The land, moreover, shall not be sold permanently, for the land is Mine; for you are but aliens and sojourners with Me.** [24] **'Thus for every piece of your property, you are to provide for the redemption of the land.**
[25] **'If a fellow countryman of yours becomes so poor he has to sell part of his property, then his nearest kinsman is to come and buy back what his relative has sold.** [26] **'Or in case a man has no kinsman, but so recovers his means as to find sufficient for its redemption,** [27] **then he shall calculate the**

years since its sale and refund the balance to the man to whom he sold it, and so return to his property.
[28] 'But if he has not found sufficient means to get it back for himself, then what he has sold shall remain in the hands of its purchaser until the year of jubilee; but at the jubilee it shall revert, that he may return to his property.
Leviticus 25:23-28 (NASB)

[47] 'Now if the means of a stranger or of a sojourner with you becomes sufficient, and a countryman of yours becomes so poor with regard to him as to sell himself to a stranger who is sojourning with you, or to the descendants of a stranger's family, [48] then he shall have redemption right after he has been sold. One of his brothers may redeem him, [49] or his uncle, or his uncle's son, may redeem him, or one of his blood relatives from his family may redeem him; or if he prospers, he may redeem himself.
Leviticus 25:47-49 (NASB)

[5] "When brothers live together and one of them dies and has no son, the wife of the deceased shall not be married outside the family to a strange man. Her husband's brother shall go in to her and take her to himself as wife and perform the duty of a husband's brother to her.
[6] "It shall be that the firstborn whom she bears shall assume the name of his dead brother, so that his name will not be blotted out from Israel.
[7] "But if the man does not desire to take his brother's wife, then his brother's wife shall go up to the gate to the elders and say, 'My husband's brother refuses to establish a name for his brother in Israel; he is not willing to perform the duty of a husband's brother to me.' [8] "Then the elders of his city shall summon him and speak to him. And if he persists and says, 'I do not desire to take her,' [9] then his

brother's wife shall come to him in the sight of the elders, and pull his sandal off his foot and spit in his face; and she shall declare, 'Thus it is done to the man who does not build up his brother's house.'
[10] "In Israel his name shall be called, 'The house of him whose sandal is removed.'
Deuteronomy 25:5-10 (NASB)

What was Ruth thinking about the rest of the night? Regardless of who that other man was, her needs for a husband would be fulfilled shortly. In addition, Naomi's poverty was also about to end, as Ruth had promised that nothing but death could separate them. Regardless of the physical exhaustion Ruth was feeling from her day harvesting barley, it is likely she did not sleep a wink, wondering if the nearer relative could be half as godly as Boaz. At the same time, Boaz also had a lot on his mind. He had finished a successful day of harvesting barley. It is likely that this work supplied the needs of many, as Boaz was a wealthy landowner. This night had been a celebration, and as was standard in those times, he slept with his harvested crops, in protection, before taking them to market. Yet now, he had another, more important issue. This godly, and likely, beautiful, young woman had miraculously come into his fields and into his life, and now, his life could be even richer with her as his wife. There was one man who stood in the way. Boaz obviously knew the man well. That night, after this discussion with Ruth, Boaz certainly weighed each outcome over and over again. Certainly, he was celebrating the harvest, but it was likely that the harvest was no longer on his mind.

So she lay at his feet until morning and rose before one could recognize another; and he said, "Let it not be known

that the woman came to the threshing floor."
Ruth 3:14 (NASB)

Both Boaz and Ruth were concerned about wagging tongues. Evil is not always the only concern; we also need to be concerned with the appearance of evil. Yet sadly, the gossip inside a church can be more pervasive than trash at a dump.

² For we all stumble in many ways. If anyone does not stumble in what he says, he is a perfect man, able to bridle the whole body as well. ³ Now if we put the bits into the horses' mouths so that they will obey us, we direct their entire body as well. ⁴ Look at the ships also, though they are so great and are driven by strong winds, are still directed by a very small rudder wherever the inclination of the pilot desires.
⁵ So also the tongue is a small part of the body, and yet it boasts of great things. See how great a forest is set aflame by such a small fire! ⁶ And the tongue is a fire, the very world of iniquity; the tongue is set among our members as that which defiles the entire body, and sets on fire the course of our life, and is set on fire by hell.
James 3:2-6 (NASB)

Boaz has godly intent in regard to Ruth, and she has godly intent in regard to Boaz. He encourages her to leave without being seen, not because either have done anything wrong. Instead, he wants to maintain his unstained reputation! Though this verse was written many years later by the apostle Paul, Boaz agreed:

Finally, brethren, whatever is true, whatever is honorable, whatever is right, whatever is pure, whatever is lovely, whatever is of good repute, if there is any excellence and if

**anything worthy of praise, dwell on these things.
Philippians 4:8**

Then Boaz does something strange; at least to us it might appear to be strange. He fills her cloak with six ephahs of barley. In dry measures, an ephah was the equivalent of four pecks or 3/5ths of a bushel. Wow, how did she carry this back to Naomi? Experts in agriculture today estimate that a bushel of barley weighs 48 pounds, so Naomi hoisted about 173 pounds of barley home to her mother-in-law! Rabbis believe that this was a message that Boaz was sending directly to Naomi, calling attention to the sixth day of the week. With *Shabbat*, the Sabbath, occurring on the seventh day, Boaz was promising to settle this issue before the Sabbath. Look closely at Ruth's comment and Naomi's response:

**[17] She said, "These six measures of barley he gave to me, for he said, 'Do not go to your mother-in-law empty-handed.' "
[18] Then she said, "Wait, my daughter, until you know how the matter turns out; for the man will not rest until he has settled it today."
Ruth 3:17-18 (NASB)**

Ruth 3 concludes with much unresolved, but Boaz is a man of resolve. What a difference a day makes, and the following day could be just as eye opening! How giddy must Ruth be feeling? After losing her husband at such a young age, she chose to leave her family, her nation and her gods. God has promised all believers that if we seek Him, we will find Him, and we can see that promise fulfilled in His relationship with Ruth. The LORD is guiding each action, and is not only answering her prayers, but the prayers of this godly landowner named Boaz. Poor Naomi had felt abandoned by Him, but God continues to care for her, though she just cannot see it. Today was special, but let's see what tomorrow brings!

DISCUSSION QUESTIONS:

1. Did Naomi plan this connection between Ruth and Boaz?
2. Boaz seemed concerned with the appearance of evil. How can we as Christians fail in this regard?
3. This appears to be a celebration of Firstfruits. Can you name another important event that occurred on the Feast of Firstfruits?
4. The gift that Boaz gave Ruth to take home to Naomi was a little odd. How do you think Ruth carried it? How do you think Naomi received it?
5. When Naomi sent Ruth out that night, was she thinking about her own need for support or was she thinking about Ruth's need for a husband?

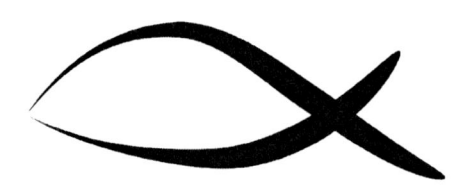

Notes:

Notes:

Chapter 6:
I've Been Redeemed

The day of redemption is at hand, what glorious words! All the characters of our story have been gathered together to complete what has begun. When did God plan this event? Before the foundations of the world! It's amazing to think that God loves each of us so much that He has planned all of the details of our lives. Though we make many sinful choices, God allows those choices and through His heavenly version of GPS (God's Positioning System), allows the brokenness from our choices to put us back on the paths He has destined for us! It is the difference between His perfect will and His permissive will. Ruth was born in Moab, a pagan nation. It is doubtful that she ever heard of the God of Abraham, but a famine in Israel brought a family of four across the Jordan River, to her nation. In that journey, they brought her future husband, and most importantly, her future God. Her father-in-law died, and then soon after, her husband and brother-in-law also died. At that moment, Ruth arrived at a fight-or-flight decision that would affect the remainder of her life. Ruth's decision to follow

Naomi, and Naomi's God, did not surprise God. Instead, the details continued to happen just as He had planned. So let's read the final chapter of the Book of Ruth, and see how God's plan continues to bless us all!

¹ Now Boaz went up to the gate and sat down there; and behold, the close relative of whom Boaz had spoken came by. So Boaz said, "Come aside, friend, sit down here." So he came aside and sat down. ² And he took ten men of the elders of the city, and said, "Sit down here." So they sat down. ³ Then he said to the close relative, "Naomi, who has come back from the country of Moab, sold the piece of land which belonged to our brother Elimelech. ⁴ And I thought to inform you, saying, 'Buy it back in the presence of the inhabitants and the elders of my people. If you will redeem it, redeem it; but if you will not redeem it, then tell me, that I may know; for there is no one but you to redeem it, and I am next after you.' " And he said, "I will redeem it." ⁵ Then Boaz said, "On the day you buy the field from the hand of Naomi, you must also buy it from Ruth the Moabitess, the wife of the dead, to perpetuate the name of the dead through his inheritance." ⁶ And the close relative said, "I cannot redeem it for myself, lest I ruin my own inheritance. You redeem my right of redemption for yourself, for I cannot redeem it."

⁷ Now this was the custom in former times in Israel concerning redeeming and exchanging, to confirm anything: one man took off his sandal and gave it to the other, and this was a confirmation in Israel. ⁸ Therefore the close relative said to Boaz, "Buy it for yourself." So he took off his sandal. ⁹ And Boaz said to the elders and all the people, "You are witnesses this day that I have bought all that was Elimelech's, and all that was Chilion's and Mahlon's, from the hand of Naomi. ¹⁰ Moreover, Ruth the

Moabitess, the widow of Mahlon, I have acquired as my wife, to perpetuate the name of the dead through his inheritance, that the name of the dead may not be cut off from among his brethren and from his position at the gate. You are witnesses this day." [11] And all the people who were at the gate, and the elders, said, "We are witnesses. The Lord make the woman who is coming to your house like Rachel and Leah, the two who built the house of Israel; and may you prosper in Ephrathah and be famous in Bethlehem. [12] May your house be like the house of Perez, whom Tamar bore to Judah, because of the offspring which the Lord will give you from this young woman."

[13] So Boaz took Ruth and she became his wife; and when he went in to her, the Lord gave her conception, and she bore a son. [14] Then the women said to Naomi, "Blessed be the Lord, who has not left you this day without a close relative; and may his name be famous in Israel! [15] And may he be to you a restorer of life and a nourisher of your old age; for your daughter-in-law, who loves you, who is better to you than seven sons, has borne him." [16] Then Naomi took the child and laid him on her bosom, and became a nurse to him. [17] Also the neighbor women gave him a name, saying, "There is a son born to Naomi." And they called his name Obed. He is the father of Jesse, the father of David. [18] Now this is the genealogy of Perez: Perez begot Hezron; [19] Hezron begot Ram, and Ram begot Amminadab; [20] Amminadab begot Nahshon, and Nahshon begot Salmon; [21] Salmon begot Boaz, and Boaz begot Obed; [22] Obed begot Jesse, and Jesse begot David.

Ruth 4:1-22 (NKJV)

Again, we need to emphasize that Ruth asked Boaz to be her kinsman redeemer (*goel*), and then Boaz, a man of action, went to town! So as our story continues, we see Boaz at the gate of the city, waiting for the nearest relative of Mahlon, Ruth's deceased husband. When visiting the old cities of Mexico, if we go to the main plaza of the city on a Saturday night, called the *zócalo*, all of the townspeople are there. In ancient Israel, all of the comings and goings occurred at the gates to the city. While Jerusalem had many gates, Bethlehem may have had fewer. Regardless, this gate where Boaz came on this special day also was where the judges of the city made decisions. By Mosaic Law, there was a specific procedure in the cases of Levirate marriage, and Boaz honors God's Law, with one interesting change. By Law, Ruth should have confronted the closer relative, but in this case, Boaz represents her and mediates the entire situation. He patiently waits at the city gate for the relative, as Boaz is a man who is filled by the Spirit of the LORD. Patience is a fruit of the Holy Spirit. It is easy to picture Boaz scanning the faces, excited about what is to happen this day, and likely, a little nervous that the other relative will want to redeem Ruth.

Finally, the man walks by, and though Boaz certainly knows him by name, he does not call the relative by name, but tells him to sit down with the 10 elders of the city. What that man must be thinking! Why is Boaz not supervising the harvest of the fields? Why is he being taken before judges? Has he done something wrong? And then Boaz begins to plead his case, in the same skillful manner of a high-priced attorney. He refers to Elimelech as "our brother," though it is doubtful that both were brothers of Elimelech. In Hebrew, this is the same term a man would use of another blood relative. We also know that Boaz was not the closest relative, which tells us that their standing was different in some way. Boaz proceeds by telling the relative that the land of Naomi, Elimelech's wife, needs to be redeemed. The relative generously agrees to fulfill that duty. But then Boaz gets to the heart of the matter. He tells the relative that Naomi's daughter-in-law, who will inherit the land, must also be redeemed. Notice what Boaz tells the relative about Ruth, only one aspect. She is a Moabitess. Also notice what Boaz does not tell him: she is beautiful, she is compassionate, she is hardworking…

The closer relative says, "I cannot redeem it for myself, lest I ruin my own inheritance. You redeem my right of redemption for yourself, for I cannot redeem it." We do not know the reason why the closer relative was unable to be the kinsman redeemer, as in the previous passages we can see that he was willing. It could be that he is already married, but it is more likely that it has to do with that one nugget of information that Boaz shared about Ruth: she is from Moab! Remember this law?

[3] **"An Ammonite or Moabite shall not enter the assembly of the Lord; even to the tenth generation none of his descendants shall enter the assembly of the Lord forever,** [4] **because they did not meet you with bread and water on the road when you came out of Egypt, and because they hired against you Balaam the son of Beor from Pethor of Mesopotamia, to curse you.** [5] **Nevertheless the Lord your God would not listen to Balaam, but the Lord your God turned the curse into a blessing for you, because the Lord your God loves you.** [6] **You shall not seek their peace nor their prosperity all your days forever.**
Deuteronomy 23:3-6 (NKJV)

This man is worried that redeeming Ruth will simultaneously jeopardize his own land and inheritance. Boaz must have had trouble hiding his joy as soon as the closer relative passed on the duty of redemption. By the Law, there were more steps, and the nearer relative removed his sandal and handed it to

Boaz. The sandal is emblematic of a man's walk. Think of what Jesus did the night of His arrest and the night before His crucifixion. He washed the feet of His disciples. When Peter questioned why Jesus would act in this servant's role, Jesus told Peter that if He did not wash their feet, they would have no part in Him! When Peter then asked for the LORD to wash all of him, Jesus told Peter that all He needed to have cleaned were his feet. Our feet carry us to every sin. Though the sins begin in our desperately wicked hearts, the feet usually have us running to that sin, once we have made our minds up. In the same manner, Joseph's feet ran far away from the advances of Potiphar's wife in Genesis 39. We have more than sandals on our feet. In ancient Israel, there was much sand and dirt to cover their feet, and the main transportation was walking. Instead of dirt, what should be on the feet of believers?

and having shod your feet with the preparation of the gospel of peace;
Ephesians 6:15 (NKJV)

Certainly, Boaz was grounded in the Word of God, and this day may have been the most peaceful one in his life! Boaz did not, however, spit in the nearer relative's face. Possibly, this had to do with the fact that the nearer relative was willing, just not able, to perform as Ruth's kinsman redeemer. All procedure had been handled according to the Law, and in front of the 10 witnesses.

Boaz announces:

[9] And Boaz said to the elders and all the people, "You are witnesses this day that I have bought all that was Elimelech's, and all that was Chilion's and Mahlon's, from the hand of Naomi. [10] Moreover, Ruth the Moabitess, the

widow of Mahlon, I have acquired as my wife, to perpetuate the name of the dead through his inheritance, that the name of the dead may not be cut off from among his brethren and from his position at the gate. You are witnesses this day."
Ruth 4:9-10 (NKJV)

This redemption cost Boaz, though we do not know the price he had to pay. Without him stepping in, Naomi would not be able to return to the land of her inheritance until the year of Jubilee, when all debts would be forgiven. But even with the cost, it was more about what Boaz received in the transaction. He gained a godly wife. The people at the gate were also witnesses and also commented:

[11] And all the people who were at the gate, and the elders, said, "We are witnesses. The Lord make the woman who is coming to your house like Rachel and Leah, the two who built the house of Israel; and may you prosper in Ephrathah and be famous in Bethlehem. [12] May your house be like the house of Perez, whom Tamar bore to Judah, because of the offspring which the Lord will give you from this young woman."
Ruth 4:11-12 (NKJV)

By mentioning Rachel and Leah, they referred to wives of Jacob, who bore eight of the 12 sons of Jacob, renamed Israel by God. Leah had Reuben, Simeon, Levi, Judah, Issachar and Zebulun, and we know that Jesus, the Messiah, came from the tribe of Judah. Rachel was the mother of Joseph and Benjamin, and when she died in childbirth with Benjamin, was buried just outside Bethlehem. Certainly, the people of Bethlehem were familiar with every aspect of the bloodlines here. Then the people make another reference, hoping that the house of Boaz, through his offspring with Ruth, become like the house of Perez. What? On the surface, that appears to be insulting! In Chapter 2 of this book, we discussed the relationship between Judah and Tamar. Tamar had been married to Judah's son Er, but the LORD took Er's life for being evil in His sight. Er's brother Onan, who was supposed to become the kinsman redeemer of his deceased brother's wife, intentionally did not give her children, and the LORD also took his life. When Judah failed to have his third son step up as Tamar's kinsman redeemer, Tamar tricked Judah, and played the role of a prostitute. She became pregnant with Judah's sons, who in a strange way were also his grandsons! These were the twins Perez and Zerah, though only Perez is mentioned in this wish of the witnesses. What was special about Perez? Why would they wish any part of this sordid affair on the house of Boaz?

The ensuing genealogy answers that question. Ruth and Boaz have a child, named Obed. Here is how the fourth chapter of Ruth concludes:

**[17] And they called his name Obed. He is the father of Jesse, the father of David. [18] Now this is the genealogy of Perez: Perez begot Hezron; [19] Hezron begot Ram, and Ram begot Amminadab; [20] Amminadab begot Nahshon, and Nahshon begot Salmon; [21] Salmon begot Boaz, and Boaz begot Obed; [22] Obed begot Jesse, and Jesse begot David.
Ruth 4:17-22 (NKJV)**

Obed was the grandfather of King David! Let's look back at these verses again to see another interesting nugget from this passage:

² **"One of illegitimate birth shall not enter the assembly of the Lord; even to the tenth generation none of his descendants shall enter the assembly of the Lord.** ³ **"An Ammonite or Moabite shall not enter the assembly of the Lord; even to the tenth generation none of his descendants shall enter the assembly of the Lord forever, Deuteronomy 23:2-3 (NKJV)**

Interesting! Though Perez and Zerah were born to unmarried parents, and were thus, illegitimate, notice that there were exactly 10 generations from Tamar to King David:

Perez, Hezron, Ram, Amminadab, Nahshon, Salmon, Boaz, Obed, Jesse, and David. God does not miss a thing!

For those who overlook the genealogies when reading the Bible, we also need to know a little more about this godly man, Boaz.

Salmon begot Boaz by Rahab, Boaz begot Obed by Ruth, Obed begot Jesse, 6 and Jesse begot David the king. Matthew 1:5 (NKJV)

Does anyone remember Rahab? With Joshua preparing to overthrow Jericho, he sent two spies into that city, and those spies were hidden and protected by the prostitute Rahab (Joshua 2). In exchange for helping the spies, they ensured her safety as well as the safety of her family when God destroyed Jericho. The LORD also destroyed every person inside the city, except for Rahab and her family. She married Salmon and raised the godly son of Boaz. While the closer relative had issues with Ruth being from Moab, Boaz did not have any problem. His mother was a prostitute, spared by God. He certainly understood God's grace!

How wonderful for all of us that God chose His Son, our Messiah, to come through the bloodline of Tamar and Judah's illegitimate child, through the prostitute Rahab and through the Moabitess Ruth, of a pagan nation. In so doing, God demonstrates that grace to each one of us! In the next chapter, we will look into the symbolism of the Book of Ruth, along with the depth of that imagery.

DISCUSSION QUESTIONS:

1. If the Law was against a Moabite entering into the assembly of the LORD, why was Boaz still willing to redeem Naomi and marry Ruth?
2. Why were the witnesses all in favor of Boaz, based on their complimentary wishes?
3. Why did the closer relative take off his sandal and hand it to Boaz? How is this tradition symbolic?
4. What is the significance of the bloodline at the end of this chapter? What should that tell us about how God views our sin when we have repented?
5. If we are God's children, is it sinful for us to worry, even if we are in stressful or seemingly hopeless situations?

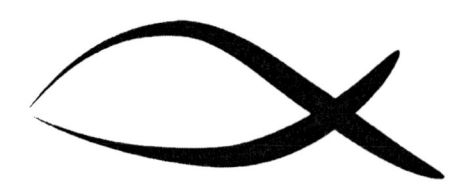

Notes:

Notes:

Chapter 7,
By the Blood of the Lamb

Now we know the story of Boaz and Ruth, and we also understand the significance and meaning of redemption, especially in reference to the Levirate marriage of the Old Testament. When studying the Bible it is personal application that makes each word come alive, makes each phrase memorable and makes it "my story" instead of "history." One of the best tools to dig deeper is inductive Bible study, with the three steps being observation, interpretation and application. In the observation stage, we ask journalistic questions without answering them. During interpretation, we try to bring in other Bible verses that are applicable to the passage we are studying. Those may include key words that occur in other locations. We also may bring in other sources, like a commentary, a dictionary or an atlas, to help fill in some of the gaps and help us to understand the passage better. In the final stage of application, we learn to apply the passage to our lives, because the Lord wants us to grow closer to Him every day. Part of that closeness is becoming more like Him, and God tells us all about Himself in the Bible. Though we never can approach His attributes, we can reflect Him! In this final chapter, let's address the symbolism involved in the Book of Ruth, which will make that personal application much easier to achieve. First of all, we need to re-examine our cast of characters:

<u>Boaz</u>: a wealthy landowner in Bethlehem. He is single and takes a Gentile bride to be his wife. In order to do so, he needs to "redeem" her. That means that he must pay all of her debts.

<u>Ruth</u>: she is the poor woman from Moab. Her husband Mahlon died, and then she left her country, her family and her gods for Israel. In Israel, she worked hard gleaning the fields of Boaz, and discovered that he was a close relative. After another closer relative could not redeem her, Ruth married Boaz. Without him, Ruth would have remained a poor Moabitess widow.

<u>Naomi</u>: she married Elimelech in Bethlehem, had two sons (Mahlon and Chilion), and when a famine hit Israel, the family moved across the Jordan River to Moab. Mahlon and Chilion both married, and sadly, Elimelech and the two sons all died in the 10 years there. Naomi returned to Bethlehem, and while daughter-in-law Orpah returned to her family, Naomi's other daughter-in-law Ruth remained with Naomi to share the journey and the rest of her life.

<u>Unnamed servant</u>: introduced Boaz to Ruth.

<u>Closer relative</u>: this unnamed man was also a relative of Elimelech, and was a closer relative than Boaz. He was willing to redeem Ruth, but was not able. He was unwilling to marry

this woman from Moab.

Orpah: the wife of Chilion. Like Ruth, she learned about the God of the Jews, and when all three women became widows, she chose to follow Naomi to Israel. Naomi tried to talk both young women into returning to their own families, and while Ruth still chose to follow her, Orpah remained in Moab.

Let's return to Boaz and review his character traits that we discussed in Chapter 4:

Character traits of Boaz:	Bible verses:
Man of great wealth	Ruth 2:1
Close relative of Elimelech	Ruth 2:1
From Bethlehem	Ruth 2:3
Worships God	Ruth 2:4
Observant	Ruth 2:11
Comforter	Ruth 2:13
Feeds the hungry	Ruth 2:14
Servant	Ruth 2:14
Protector	Ruth 2:15
Provider	Ruth 2:16

These character traits should remind us of someone we know well...Jesus! He is our *goel*, our Kinsman Redeemer! Our only real wealth comes from Him, for if we know Jesus as Lord and Savior, we are rich beyond measure. Once He puts us under His wing, we are adopted as children of God, and retain the same rights of inheritance given Him by the Father:

**Therefore I will divide Him a portion with the great,
And He shall divide the spoil with the strong,**

**Because He poured out His soul unto death,
And He was numbered with the transgressors,
And He bore the sin of many,
And made intercession for the transgressors.
Isaiah 53:12 (NKJV)**

Just like Boaz, Jesus was born in Bethlehem, and notice some of those other traits, as well. He is the Comforter. When Jesus returned to heaven, He promised to leave "another" in His place. That word for "another" in Greek was *allos*, which means another of the same kind, as opposed to *heteros*, which means another of a different kind. We know that Comforter refers to the Holy Spirit, but God is One and that is also an attribute of Jesus! Just as Boaz fed Ruth, Jesus feeds the hungry. While this can point to the miraculous feedings he accomplished when He walked on this earth as a man, more importantly, it points to the only food that can feed our souls. He is the Bread of life (John 6:35). Amazingly, this points back to His birthplace as Bethlehem means, "house of bread." Jesus was not born in Bethlehem by accident! Just as Boaz served Ruth, Jesus came as the Servant of all. Remember the night before He was crucified when our LORD washed the feet of the disciples. Peter, in particular, was extremely uncomfortable with Jesus performing as a servant. Finally, He is our Protector and Provider. Jesus fights our battles for us and provides all of our needs. Just as Boaz paid all of Ruth and Naomi's debts, Jesus paid for our debts on the cross!

Remember that Boaz represented Ruth when going to meet the closer relative, which was different than the Levirate marriage law of the Old Testament where the one to be redeemed did the confronting. This points to Jesus, who goes to the Father on our behalves. Even now, He sits at God's right hand and mediates for us! So if Jesus is the Kinsman Redeemer, who is

Ruth? She is the Gentile bride. Remember, Jesus came to save the Jews first:

> [21] **Then Jesus went out from there and departed to the region of Tyre and Sidon.** [22] **And behold, a woman of Canaan came from that region and cried out to Him, saying, "Have mercy on me, O Lord, Son of David! My daughter is severely demon-possessed."**
> [23] **But He answered her not a word. And His disciples came and urged Him, saying, "Send her away, for she cries out after us."**
> [24] **But He answered and said, "I was not sent except to the lost sheep of the house of Israel."**
> **Matthew 15:21-24 (NKJV)**

Jesus shared a parable of a wedding feast, when the people who were invited chose not to attend. Instead of celebrating without guests, though, new guests were invited. Because the Jews did not answer His call, Jesus invited the Gentiles, and held the Jews accountable for not knowing when He was coming:

> [41] **Now as He drew near, He saw the city and wept over it,** [42] **saying, "If you had known, even you, especially in this your day, the things that make for your peace! But now they are hidden from your eyes.** [43] **For days will come upon you when your enemies will build an embankment around you, surround you and close you in on every side,** [44] **and level you, and your children within you, to the ground; and they will not leave in you one stone upon another, because you did not know the time of your visitation."**
> **Luke 19:41-44 (NKJV)**

We need to remember that this invitation to Gentiles was part of God's plan, and that His plan also includes another time for the Jews to accept Him as Lord and Savior. The Bible speaks of the "fullness of the Gentiles," (Romans 11:25) and in the Great Tribulation, one-third of the Jews on the earth will accept Jesus as Messiah (Zechariah 13:8). Ruth, the Gentile bride of the Kinsman Redeemer, gave us an Old Testament symbol of Jesus' calling to the Gentile.

[1] And Jesus answered and spoke to them again by parables and said: [2] "The kingdom of heaven is like a certain king who arranged a marriage for his son, [3] and sent out his servants to call those who were invited to the wedding; and they were not willing to come. [4] Again, he sent out other servants, saying, 'Tell those who are invited, "See, I have prepared my dinner; my oxen and fatted cattle are killed, and all things are ready. Come to the wedding." ' [5] But they made light of it and went their ways, one to his own farm, another to his business. [6] And the rest seized his servants, treated them spitefully, and killed them. [7] But when the king heard about it, he was furious. And he sent out his armies, destroyed those murderers, and burned up their city. [8] Then he said to his servants, 'The wedding is ready, but those who were invited were not worthy. [9] Therefore go into the highways, and as many as you find, invite to the wedding.' [10] So those servants went out into the highways and gathered together all whom they found, both bad and good. And the wedding hall was filled with guests.
[11] "But when the king came in to see the guests, he saw a man there who did not have on a wedding garment. [12] So he said to him, 'Friend, how did you come in here without a wedding garment?' And he was speechless. [13] Then the king said to the servants, 'Bind him hand and foot, take him away, and cast him into outer darkness; there will be weeping and gnashing of teeth.'

[14] **"For many are called, but few are chosen."**
Matthew 22:1-14 (NKJV)

Just as the closer relative was unwilling to redeem Ruth, Boaz could also have passed on this Moabite. Though lovely and sweet, the redemption of Ruth by Boaz involved grace. This grace was easier for Boaz than for many others if we understand His ancestry. Remember, his mother was Rahab the harlot, the prostitute who was spared from God's destruction on Jericho for hiding the Jewish spies!

Let's look closer at Ruth's character traits discussed in Chapter 4:

Character Traits of Ruth:	Bible Verse:
From Moab	Ruth 2:2
Poor	Ruth 2:2
Hard worker	Ruth 2:7
Good listener	Ruth 2:8
Thankful	Ruth 2:10
Compassionate	Ruth 2:11
Seeker of God	Ruth 2:12
Hungry	Ruth 2:14
Sharer	Ruth 2:18
Provider	Ruth 2:18

She was from Moab, symbolic of the nations. Moab did not seek the LORD, but instead, worshipped a variety of idols. That should remind each of us of our walks before we heard the calling of Jesus! Ruth was poor, and so were each of us, without Him. Wealth has nothing to do with earthly possessions, but instead, the position of God in our lives as our

Provider. Ruth was a hard worker and a good listener. When we come to the LORD, we have His salvation, but in order to draw closer to Him, that involves a relationship. There cannot be a viable relationship without some diligent labor. Our LORD does not ask us to sit on our backsides after meeting Him, but to get busy in His work! Also notice that Ruth was thankful. There is probably not an uglier trait than unthankfulness, and it is sad how much the LORD does for His children that receives no thanks. When Jesus healed the 10 lepers in Luke 17:11-19, only one man returned to thank Him! In Ruth's dealings with Boaz, she is a great example of how each believer should be with Jesus, revealing a thankful heart.

Seeing Ruth's compassion for Naomi spoke so loudly to the heart of Boaz, and as we later will discuss the symbolism of Naomi, do not lose sight of that same compassion that believers can share. How can a believer not be compassionate, when each of us should see ourselves before we knew Jesus when looking at unbelievers? While Ruth's compassion might have convinced Boaz to redeem her, Boaz would not have done so without her seeking him. God tells us numerous times in the Bible how important it is for us to seek Him. Let's look at a few of those:

7 "Ask, and it will be given to you; seek, and you will find; knock, and it will be opened to you. 8 For everyone who asks receives, and he who seeks finds, and to him who knocks it will be opened.
Matthew 7:7-8 (NKJV)

Draw near to God and He will draw near to you. Cleanse your hands, you sinners; and purify your hearts, you double-minded.
James 4:8 (NKJV)

**And you will seek Me and find Me, when you search for Me with all your heart.
Jeremiah 29:13 (NKJV)**

Ruth did diligently seek Boaz, and as Christians, we need to diligently seek the LORD. In a game of hide-and-seek, how can we find the person hiding if we do not look for them? God wants for us to find Him. If we are the seeker in a game of hide-and-seek, He would be the One hiding behind the lamp in the middle of room!

Why did Ruth seek Boaz? Naomi led her to the fields of Boaz, and Ruth was hungry. Unless each person realizes that life without the LORD is the saddest version of failure, why would they seek Jesus? When we are hungry, we search for food, but some are willing to eat the smallest morsels, just as Ruth gleaned the fields of Boaz for mere existence. Yet God desires for us to go the next level in our relationships with Him, just as Ruth became the bride of Boaz.

We are the brides of Christ! God gave man the covenant of marriage so we could understand the intimacy He desires with each of us. This is not the physcial intimacy of the marital bed, but Jesus desires for us to be more intimate with Him than we can be, or could ever be, with anyone else! How sad it is that in our modern culture, we easily share that intimacy with so many others. Let's look to the future:

[7] Let us be glad and rejoice and give Him glory, for the marriage of the Lamb has come, and His wife has made herself ready." [8] And to her it was granted to be arrayed in fine linen, clean and bright, for the fine linen is the righteous acts of the saints. [9] Then he said to me, "Write: 'Blessed are those who are called to the marriage supper of

**the Lamb!' " And he said to me, "These are the true sayings of God."
Revelation 19:7-9 (NKJV)**

Naomi, on the other hand, is symbolic of the nation of Israel. When Boaz redeemed Ruth, he also redeemed Naomi. In the same manner, God will redeem Israel. Jesus came to save them. The Father chose the nation of Israel, chose the Jews and chose to be their God. None of those decisions were accidental. When faced with the death of her husband, the death of her sons and the alienation of being in a foreign land, Naomi felt abandoned by God. Israel never has been abandoned by God. Israel is the apple of the Lord's eye! The Jews are God's chosen people!

After the crucifixion of Jesus, the Temple was destroyed by the Romans in A.D. 70. At that time, the Jews were spread to the four corners of the world. Miraculously, in 1948, Israel once again became a nation. Hebrew, which had been a dead language, began to be spoken again, as the Jews returned to Israel. In 1967, the Jews re-inhabited Jerusalem. Does this sound like a nation abandoned by God?

**[8] For thus says the LORD of hosts: "He sent Me after glory, to the nations which plunder you; for he who touches you touches the apple of His eye. [9] For surely I will shake My hand against them, and they shall become spoil for their servants. Then you will know that the LORD of hosts has sent Me.
[10] "Sing and rejoice, O daughter of Zion! For behold, I am coming and I will dwell in your midst," says the LORD.
[11] "Many nations shall be joined to the LORD in that day, and they shall become My people. And I will dwell in your midst. Then you will know that the LORD of hosts has sent**

Me to you. ¹² **And the LORD will take possession of Judah as His inheritance in the Holy Land, and will again choose Jerusalem.** ¹³ **Be silent, all flesh, before the LORD, for He is aroused from His holy habitation!"**
Zechariah 2:8-13 (NKJV)

Just as the Gospel spread to the Gentiles after the Diaspora, Naomi did not return to the land of Israel until the bride was ready. Could that mean that the Wedding Supper of the Lamb is around the corner? At the very least, since the Jews returned to the land of Israel, we know that the last days have begun. That does not mean that the world will end tomorrow, for by God's standards a day is like a thousand years and a thousand years like a day. But we know his promises are at hand!

An overlooked aspect of symbolism in this lovely romance is the head servant of Boaz, who was over all the reapers. It was he who introduced Ruth to Boaz. That unnamed man promised Boaz that he would protect Ruth, too. Who is the unnamed servant who introduced each of us to Jesus? The Holy Spirit! In Genesis 24, Abraham sends his unnamed servant to find a bride for his son Isaac. That servant found Rebekah in Nahor, modern-day Turkey according to most scholars, and brought back the bride to God's chosen land. In the same manner, God sent His unnamed servant of the Holy Spirit to the Gentiles, who brings us to Jesus! Notice that the Holy Spirit never testifies of Himself!

Another unnamed and significant person in the account of Boaz and Ruth is the closer relative, who could not redeem Ruth. Symbolically, he is the Law. God gave the Law to the Jews, and along with it, the sacrificial system. But the Law could not redeem the Jews. For us, Jesus has accomplished what the Law could not! Because each of us are sinners, and the wages of sin is death, Jesus became sin for us. He carried our sins, received the death we earned, and redeemed us with the most precious price of His blood.

For He made Him who knew no sin to be sin for us, that we might become the righteousness of God in Him.
2 Corinthians 5:21 (NKJV)

Jesus did not come from the tribe of Levi, which God set aside as His priests. Instead, He was from the tribe of Judah:

[14] For it is evident that our Lord arose from Judah, of which tribe Moses spoke nothing concerning priesthood. [15] And it is yet far more evident if, in the likeness of Melchizedek, there arises another priest [16] who has come, not according to the law of a fleshly commandment, but according to the power of an endless life. [17] For He testifies:

**"You are a priest forever
According to the order of Melchizedek."**

[18] For on the one hand there is an annulling of the former commandment because of its weakness and unprofitableness, [19] for the law made nothing perfect; on the other hand, there is the bringing in of a better hope, through which we draw near to God.
Hebrews 7:14-19 (NKJV)

The Book of Ruth demonstrates grace, instead of the Law! By the Law, Boaz would not have married Ruth. By Law, Boaz would have allowed Ruth to glean in his fields, but that would have been the limit. By Law, Naomi would have waited for the Year of Jubilee or her death for any rest. Grace overlooks all of our shortcomings, as they are covered by the blood of the

Lamb! Grace accomplished what the Law could not:

> [24] **Therefore the law was our tutor to bring us to Christ, that we might be justified by faith. [25] But after faith has come, we are no longer under a tutor.**
> **Galatians 3:24-25**

Even after the redemption of Ruth, Naomi was the nurse of Obed. In the same manner, we do not cast the Law away, but we keep the Law because of our love for our Redeemer, for His grace and for His mercy!

Orpah is the saddest character in our story. She married into a family that knew the LORD, and when her husband died, she decided to follow her mother-in-law to Israel. Sadly, Ruth talked her out of it, and she returned to her family, and most sadly, returned to her gods. She is a symbol of all the people who hear the calling of Jesus, but do not heed that call! They may even know that there is a huge hole in their hearts, but instead of choosing Him, they choose something else to fill that hole.

> [13] **"Enter by the narrow gate; for wide is the gate and broad is the way that leads to destruction, and there are many who go in by it. [14] Because narrow is the gate and difficult is the way which leads to life, and there are few who find it.**
> **Matthew 7:13-14 (NKJV)**

As we wrap this chapter up, we need to look at the way the book ends, with a discussion of genealogy:

> [13] **So Boaz took Ruth and she became his wife; and when he went in to her, the LORD gave her conception, and she bore a son. [14] Then the women said to Naomi, "Blessed be**

the LORD, who has not left you this day without a close relative; and may his name be famous in Israel! [15] And may he be to you a restorer of life and a nourisher of your old age; for your daughter-in-law, who loves you, who is better to you than seven sons, has borne him." [16] Then Naomi took the child and laid him on her bosom, and became a nurse to him. [17] Also the neighbor women gave him a name, saying, "There is a son born to Naomi." And they called his name Obed. He is the father of Jesse, the father of David.
[18] Now this is the genealogy of Perez: Perez begot Hezron; [19] Hezron begot Ram, and Ram begot Amminadab; [20] Amminadab begot Nahshon, and Nahshon begot Salmon; [21] Salmon begot Boaz, and Boaz begot Obed; [22] Obed begot Jesse, and Jesse begot David.
Ruth 4:13-22 (NKJV)

Here, we see that the child of Boaz and Ruth was the grandfather of King David. In this beautiful, Old Testament, historic tale, we see the beginning of the kings of Israel. Saul was man's king, but David was God's king. And most importantly, this was the bloodline of Jesus, the King of kings and the LORD of lords. Let's look at that bloodline from Abraham in the Gospel of Matthew:

[1] **The record of the genealogy of Jesus the Messiah, the son of David, the son of Abraham:**
[2] **Abraham was the father of Isaac, Isaac the father of Jacob, and Jacob the father of Judah and his brothers.**
[3] **Judah was the father of Perez and Zerah by Tamar, Perez was the father of Hezron, and Hezron the father of Ram.**
[4] **Ram was the father of Amminadab, Amminadab the father of Nahshon, and Nahshon the father of Salmon.**
[5] **Salmon was the father of Boaz by Rahab, Boaz was the father of Obed by Ruth, and Obed the father of Jesse.**

⁶ Jesse was the father of David the king.
David was the father of Solomon by Bathsheba who had been the wife of Uriah.
⁷ Solomon was the father of Rehoboam, Rehoboam the father of Abijah, and Abijah the father of Asa.
⁸ Asa was the father of Jehoshaphat, Jehoshaphat the father of Joram, and Joram the father of Uzziah.
⁹ Uzziah was the father of Jotham, Jotham the father of Ahaz, and Ahaz the father of Hezekiah.
¹⁰ Hezekiah was the father of Manasseh, Manasseh the father of Amon, and Amon the father of Josiah.
¹¹ Josiah became the father of Jeconiah and his brothers, at the time of the deportation to Babylon.
¹² After the deportation to Babylon: Jeconiah became the father of Shealtiel, and Shealtiel the father of Zerubbabel.
¹³ Zerubbabel was the father of Abihud, Abihud the father of Eliakim, and Eliakim the father of Azor.
¹⁴ Azor was the father of Zadok, Zadok the father of Achim, and Achim the father of Eliud.
¹⁵ Eliud was the father of Eleazar, Eleazar the father of Matthan, and Matthan the father of Jacob.
¹⁶ Jacob was the father of Joseph the husband of Mary, by whom Jesus was born, who is called the Messiah.
¹⁷ So all the generations from Abraham to David are fourteen generations; from David to the deportation to Babylon, fourteen generations; and from the deportation to Babylon to the Messiah, fourteen generations.
Matthew 1:1-17 (NKJV)

In verse four above, we see Perez, the son of Tamar and Judah, the result of when Tamar played the harlot. In verse five above, we see Boaz and Ruth and their son Obed. In Matthew, we see the legal line of Christ, from Abraham to David, continuing through Solomon and the royal line to Joseph, Jesus' legal father. However, in Luke 3, Luke focuses on the humanity of Jesus, and not just his Jewish roots. Luke traces the bloodline back to Adam, and the two bloodlines converge from Abraham to David. Yet instead of going through Solomon, Luke traces the bloodline through Nathan, another son of David. He continues to Heli, the father of Mary. Both bloodlines show Jesus as the Lion of the tribe of Judah!

Finally, let's look closely at the names of our characters and the meaning of those names in Hebrew:

Name:	Hebrew:	Meaning
Boaz	בעז	Strength
Ruth	רות	Beauty
Obed	עובד	Worship
Naomi	נעמי	Pleasure
Mahlon	מחלון	Sickly
Chilion	כליון	Puny or wasting away
Elimelech	אלימלך	My God is King

Ray Stedman puts this together in such a wonderful way:

"Boaz means 'strength of wealth.' Elimelech means 'my God is King.' Obed means 'worship.' Naomi means 'pleasure.' Ruth means 'beauty.' So when Elimelech (my god is King) married Naomi (pleasure), he fell into the bitterness of death. Out of that comes Ruth, in the beauty of humility, taking her place as a destitute stranger, dependent upon the grace of Boaz (the strong one). He redeems her and binds her to himself in marriage. When beauty is married to strength, the house is filled with worship (the meaning of their son Obed's name.)"

The book's title comes from the Hebrew meaning of Boaz and Ruth. Only through the strength of Jesus, do we become beautiful in His sight.

Honor and majesty are before Him;
Strength and beauty are in His sanctuary.
Psalm 96:6 (NKJV)

DISCUSSION QUESTIONS:

1. As Christians, we can glean the fields or dine with the King of kings, just as Ruth experienced both. In our relationship with Jesus, what takes us from gleaning to dining at His table? What takes us from dining at His table to gleaning?
2. Discuss the differences between Law and grace. Sometimes, we can walk so strongly in grace that we ignore our own sin. Other times, we get "legalistic," especially in regard to the sin of others. How should we walk the line between Law and grace?
3. It is interesting that God chose the bloodline of Christ to go through Tamar, who played the role of a harlot; Rahab, the harlot of Jericho, and Ruth, a Gentile from Moab. What does this tell us?
4. How do you think other Jews in Bethlehem viewed this marriage between Boaz and Ruth?
5. This tale of redemption should be life-changing for us all. Who is beyond the LORD's redemption?

Notes:

Acknowledgements:

How interesting life becomes after coming to the LORD! He gives all of us different talents and abilities, and we glorify Him by using those gifts. Some of my friends have encouraged me to continue writing and teaching. That encouragement has helped me get off my backside of laziness, and placed me onto my backside, behind a computer screen. When studying and writing, I feel the LORD's pleasure, and it feels like what I am supposed to do. In closing, I want to thank a handful of friends, who God has used immensely in my life. Thanks to Todd Williams, and his family. As I have said many times, when I get to heaven, I will thank Todd for the seeds planted and watered for my salvation to occur, but even since that time, he continues to support and encourage each new project for the LORD. Thanks to Jeff Kirst, as his iron sharpens my iron on almost a daily basis. It seems like that we can discuss the Bible for hours, and he never tires of my verbosity. I would also like to thank Dave Rann, whose deep heart for God touches me and so many others. Thanks for holding up my tired arms! God put me in a family with three sisters and a step-sister, but He gave me these brothers to keep me sharp.

I also would like to thank Tom Thorne and Anthony Herron. Tom is a regular student, and a teacher cannot teach without a student. Thanks for your diligence. Anthony started my journey of learning Hebrew, and God placed us in close proximity to each other. Let's keep fighting the battles together. To God be the glory!

As I conclude this book, I was thinking about *Moab*. As I stated earlier, that means "of the Father" in Hebrew. That reminds me of the miracle God performed for me and my earthly father. For years, we did not speak. Anger, bitterness and at least on my part, hatred, were a large part of that. After becoming a Christian, and understanding how much God had forgiven in my life, I reached out to meet with my Dad. God had drawn him closer, as well. Instead of discussing all the pains, we decided to just forgive each other. Our relationship improved immensely, but God still had more in store for us.

A couple years later, I went on a week-long camping and photography trip through Arizona and Utah at Thanksgiving. On the Tuesday before Thanksgiving, I took a photo in Moab, Utah, of the Delicate Arch, and in the dark, began to set up my tent. I heard the still, small voice of God say, "Honor your Father." No, it was not audible, but I felt it so strongly! Instead of setting up camp, I loaded the truck and began driving. Moab is on Interstate-70, and my Dad lives in Kansas City, 17 hours further down Interstate-70. Late that night I got to Denver. I slept for a few hours, then began driving again. It was the day before Thanksgiving. I called my step-mother, a godly woman who I love dearly, and told her I was driving in and not to tell Dad. I expected to be there around 5 p.m., and she said he was having a medical procedure that they would tell me about later, but they should be back by 5:00.

I pulled in at 5:00 and though happy to see me, Dad seemed less than energetic. I put my clothes in the guest room, used the rest room, and 10 minutes later, sat down for dinner. Moments later, we heard a crash in the bathroom. Dad had fallen. I went in and he was on the floor, covered in blood. He asked for me to help him up and as I tried, I saw his eyes roll back in his head. I told his wife to call 911 and he was again conscious and said not to. I overruled him, and the paramedics came. In the medical procedure, they had cauterized the area of the procedure, but he had continued to bleed, and had lost a lot of blood. In fact, his blood pressure was so low that he was in danger of a stroke. If I had not been there, he might have convinced his wife not to call 911. He might have died.

The next day, we talked, and I reminded him that God never made mistakes. Consequently, we both had something to learn in this situation. "What did you learn, Dad," I asked. "I learned how much you love me," he said. And interestingly, that is exactly what I learned -- how much I love him. What a gift God gave that day. It began with a subtle prodding to drive 17 hours. If I had not listened, or even would have waited an hour before acting, I would have missed it.

When I returned home, I spoke with an old friend I had grown up with in North Carolina, Pat Penuel. When I began to tell him of what occurred, Pat started crying. He had to call me back later. When he did, Pat was still crying. He told me another part of the miracle. Knowing how rocky my relationship with my Dad had been, after Pat and another childhood friend, Mark Warren, had buried their Christian fathers, they began to pray for my relationship with my Dad. They never told me about that, but we know the power of prayer, especially of a righteous man.

"**But you, when you pray, go into your inner room, close your door and pray to your Father who is in secret, and your Father who sees what is done in secret will reward you.**
Matthew 6:6 (NKJV)

I had no idea they were praying, but God honored their compassion and answered their prayers. My story increased their faith, as well, for we all need to remember that God listens to our prayers, and answers them! Thanks, men of God, and thanks LORD, for restoring my relationship with my Dad. What a blessing, and it all started in a place named, "of the Father!"

There is no bigger miracle than redemption. Through the blood of Christ, we are new creations. Old things are passed away -- bad memories, hatred and our forgiven sin. Ruth knew this redemption. So do I! If you do not, I can tell you how to find it!

gg4jesus@gmail.com
www.garryglaub.com

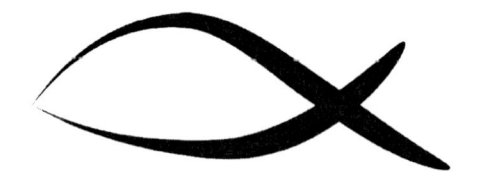

CPSIA information can be obtained
at www.ICGtesting.com
Printed in the USA
FFOW02n2037070718
47318619-50320FF